Excel 365 - 100 Tips + Tricks -

For beginners and experienced users of all ages!

100 easy step-by-step instructions containing 420 images

Book number: B3

For Windows

Author: Peter Kynast

Imprint

Bibliographic information published by the Deutsche Nationalbibliothek. The Deutsche Nationalbibliothek lists this publication in the Deutsche Nationalbibliografie; detailed bibliographic data is available on the internet at http://dnb.dnb.de.

ityco
Easy computer books
Peter Kynast
Hochstraße 14
33615 Bielefeld
Germany

Phone: +49 521 61846
Internet: www.ityco.com
Email: info@ityco.com

Image credit
stock.adobe.com - Image number: 661508081 - deagreez

134

ISBN: 979-8-32900212-6
Independently Published

First edition, June 2024, © Peter Kynast

Introduction

Dear reader,

Welcome to Excel 365 - 100 Tips + Tricks - Part 1!

This book contains 100 short instructions with many tips and tricks about Excel. This collection is based on my 24 years of experience as an IT trainer and author and will make your work with Excel much easier.

You should have a basic knowledge of Excel, then you will have a lot of fun with this book as a beginner. However, advanced users will also find many new suggestions and aids here. It is best to look at the table of contents before making your purchase decision to assess the usefulness of this book for you.

This book is localized for the US market, but you can easily use these instructions in any other region if your Excel installation is set to the English language. Dollar values inside sample files might be automatically displayed with your regional currency symbol and your standard printing paper might differ from the US letter format, but these differences will not change any steps for the instructions in this book.

To make learning as easy as possible for you, the exercises are, as always, described step by step and supplemented by over 420 images. This book is self-explanatory and the language is easy to understand - that is a promise! This will make it easy for you to memorize the new knowledge quickly. In this way, you will experience many successes and have an easy time increasing your Microsoft Excel skills.

Now I wish you lots of fun and success with Excel 365!

Best regards

Peter Kynast

Table of contents

100 Tips + Tricks

Contents

- general information
- downloading sample files
- ways to quickly enter data
- useful key combinations
- important mouse and window techniques
- easy navigation inside tables
- fast selecting and formatting
- hidden functions
- helpful control options
- and much more

General information

Please read the following notes on this book carefully.

Prerequisites

To work with this book, your computer should be equipped with Microsoft Windows 10 or 11 and Excel 365. Basic knowledge of Microsoft Windows is required.

Target audience

This book is a guide for self-learning and for Excel training courses. It is aimed at people who already have basic knowledge of Excel and are looking for tips and tricks.

Contents

- general information
- downloading sample files
- ways to quickly enter data
- useful key combinations
- important mouse and window techniques
- easy navigation inside tables
- fast selecting and formatting
- hidden functions
- helpful control options and much more

Repetitions

New topics are described in detail several times in this book and illustrated clearly. After a few repetitions, the procedure is assumed to be familiar and is therefore only reproduced in abbreviated form. Pictures are reduced in size or omitted completely.

Language

Part of good linguistic expression is to vary terms. In this way, repetition of words can be avoided and the texts become varied and lively. This golden rule of language can be a hindrance to learning processes. Learning the technical terms of a new topic is already time-consuming. Add to this their substitutes and learning success becomes unnecessarily difficult. For better understanding, this training document therefore deliberately dispenses with a certain amount of linguistic diversity. However, necessary technical terms are used and explained to an appropriate extent.

Highlighting

Emphasized terms are <u>underlined</u> or shown in ***bold and italics***. Comments on individual work steps are introduced with one of the following terms:

Attention: Indicates a possible problem.
Example: Describes an example.
Result: Explains the change that occurs because of the current work step.
Advice: Provides further explanations and information.
Or: Shows another, equivalent way.
Read more: Refers to a chapter with further explanations.

Instruction: Downloading sample files

You will need the corresponding sample files for the following instructions. You can download them from the ityco website. These instructions describe this process.

Instruction

Opening browser

1. Open the browser of your choice, e.g. *Edge, Chrome* or *Firefox*.

Advice: Edge is used in this instruction because it is most likely already installed on your computer alongside Windows. However, this process can also be carried out with any other browser.

Opening the ityco website

2. Enter the address *www.ityco.com* into the address bar.

3. Press the *enter key* ⏎ to open the website.

Downloading sample files

4. Click on the *Files* button to open the page with the sample files.

5. Scroll to the book *Excel 365 - Tips + Tricks - Part 1 - B3* to access the sample files of this book.

Excel 365 – 100 Tips + Tricks – Part 1 – B3 ⬅

Chapter 05 – Vehicle invoice – B3
Chapter 06 – Consumption – B3
Chapter 07 – Car sales – Start – B3
Chapter 07 – Car sales – Result – B3
Chapter 08 – Price conversions – B3
Chapter 10 – Computer – B3
Chapter 13 – Checking account – Start – B3
Chapter 13 – Checking account – Result – B3

---

6. Scroll down slightly further until you see the link *Excel 365 - 100 Tips + Tricks - Part 1 - B3 - Download all sample files as a ZIP file*. Click on this link to download the file.

Chapter 95 – Amusement park – B3
Chapter 97 – Tools – Start – B3
Chapter 97 – Tools – Result – B3
Chapter 98 – Fairgoers – B3
Chapter 99 – Vacation request form – Start – B3
Chapter 99 – Vacation request form – Result – B3

Excel 365 – 100 Tips + Tricks – Part 1 – B3 – Download all sample files as a ZIP file ⬅

Result: The file is downloaded and stored inside the *Downloads* folder.
Attention: Are you using Firefox? A window <u>may</u> appear asking whether you want to open the file directly or save it first. Select the *Save file* option here. Otherwise, you may have problems finding the file again later.

7. Click on the *Close* button ❌ to close the browser.
8. Click on the yellow folder icon 📁 on the taskbar to open the *Explorer*.

Or: Press the keyboard shortcut *Windows* ⊞ + E to open the Explorer.
Advice: The Explorer gives you access to files and folders on your computer. Explorer is therefore the most important app for your daily work.

---

9. Click on the **Downloads** folder to open it.

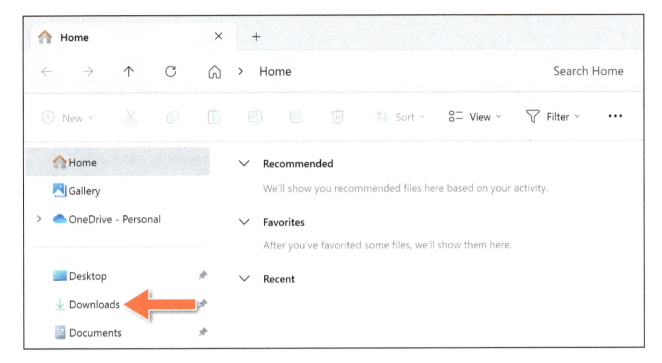

Unpacking ZIP files

The sample files are bundled in a so-called ZIP file. This combining is also called zipping or packing. To work with the sample files, you should unzip the ZIP file first. Unpacking is also known as unzipping or extracting.

10. Look at the downloaded ZIP file.

Advice: ZIP files are displayed as a folder icon with a zipper. You can see the **Compressed (zipped) Folder** description in the **Type** column.

11. Right-click on the ZIP file to open the context menu.

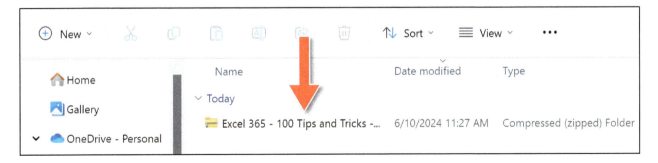

12. Click on the **Extract All** list item in the context menu to start extracting (unzipping).

Result: The **Extract Compressed (Zipped) Folders** dialog box is displayed.

13. Click on the **Show extracted files when complete** checkbox to disable this option.

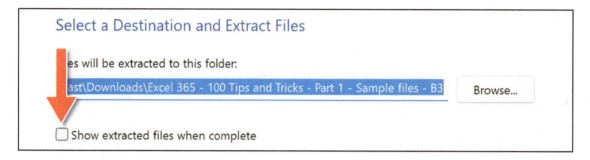

Advice: Extracting creates another folder. It contains the extracted sample files. If this box is checked when extracting, this folder will be opened automatically.

14. Click on the **Extract** button to start the extraction.

Result: The ZIP file is extracted (unzipped). The **Extract Compressed (Zipped) Folders** dialog box is then closed automatically.

15. Look at the result. You may need to scroll with the mouse to see the extracted sample file folder.

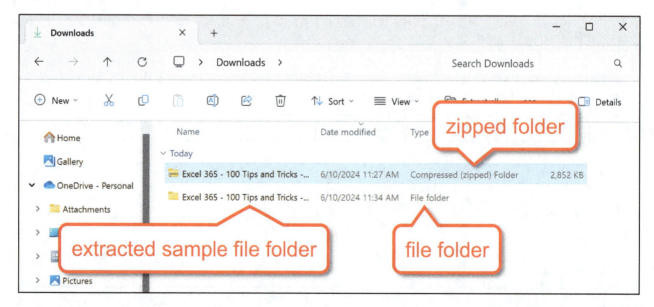

Deleting the ZIP file

The ZIP file and the folder are only slightly different. It is therefore advisable to delete the ZIP file. This way you avoid confusion when working through the exercises. If you wish, you can download the ZIP file from the website again at any time.

16. Right-click on the ZIP file.

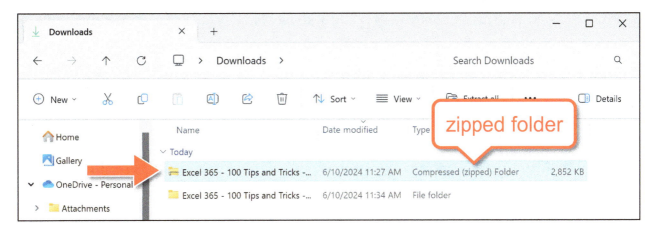

17. Click on the **Delete** button to delete the ZIP file.

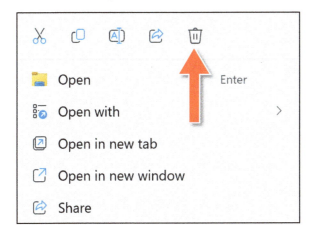

Attention: If you are working with Windows 10, the **Delete** command is <u>not</u> displayed as a recycling bin icon, but as a word in the list instead.

18. Close the **Explorer** and continue with the next chapter.

Do you need help?

Do you have any questions about this book or Excel? Write us an email and we will be happy to help you personally! Please also look at our homepage on the internet. We have prepared some help topics for you there.

Email: info@ityco.com

Internet: www.ityco.com → Help

1   Entering the current date using a key combination

Use these instructions to insert the current date using a key combination.

Instruction

1. Open Excel with an empty workbook.
2. Press the key combination **control key** `Ctrl` + **semicolon key** `;` to insert the current date.

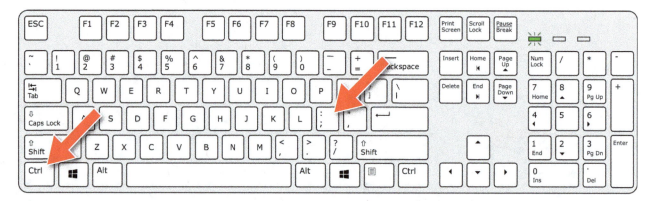

Advice: The following applies to button combinations: Hold down the first button and briefly press the second button. Then release the first button again.

3. Look at the result.

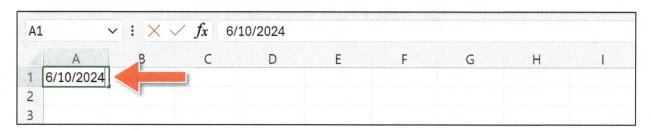

Result: The current date is entered.

4. Press the **enter key** `↵` to confirm the entry.

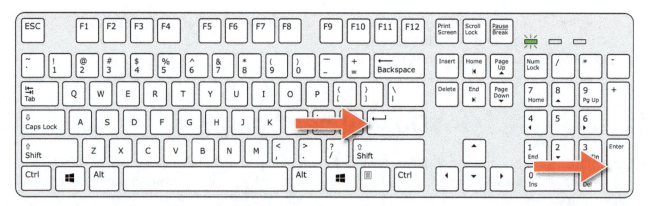

Advice: If your keyboard has a numeric keypad, the enter key is duplicated on your keyboard. The two keys are <u>identical</u> but are often labeled differently. You are free to decide which of the two keys you want to use.

5. Close Excel without saving.

2   Entering a date using the numeric keypad

Dates can be written in a variety of ways. The standard format for dates uses forward slashes, for example 4/17/2024. Using the minus sign (-) is also possible and upon entry, the format is automatically corrected to using forward slashes. Using the numeric keypad is a fast and safe way to enter date.

Instruction

1. Open Excel with an empty workbook.
2. Enter the date **4/17/24**. Enter the date by solely using the numeric keypad. Use the **forward slash key** [/] on the numeric keypad.

Advice: The numeric keypad is often abbreviated as **numpad**.

3. Look at the data entry.

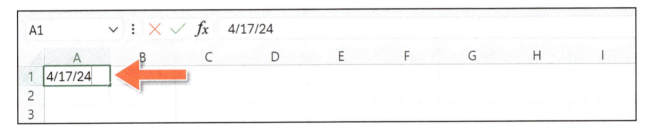

4. Confirm the entry using the **enter key** [↵] on the numpad and look at the result again.

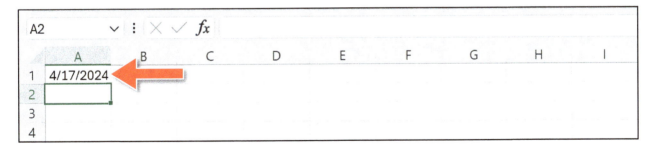

Result: The input is automatically converted to the date format **4/17/2024**. The year 24 is automatically corrected to 2024.

Advice: You can also use the minus sign (-) instead of forward slashes to enter dates.

5. Close Excel without saving.

3   Inserting a dynamic date

Use these instructions to create a dynamic date.

Instruction

1. Open Excel with an empty workbook.
2. Enter the function **=TODAY()** in a cell.

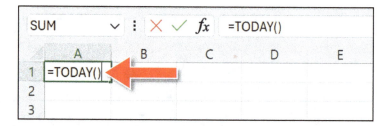

3. Press the **enter key** ↵ and look at the result.

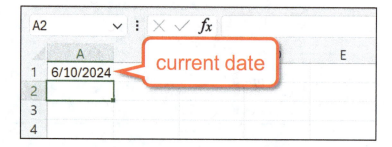

Result: The **=TODAY()** function generates the current date.

Advice: The image above was created on 6/10/2024, therefore it shows the date 6/10/2024. When you enter this function in Excel, your current date will be displayed. This function is updated every day and always shows the current date. You can also calculate with this function. If you always want to display tomorrow's date, you can use the formula **=TODAY()+1**.

4. Close Excel without saving.

4   Preventing automatic formatting changes

In some situations, Excel automatically changes the input and displays something other than what you have entered. This often happens with dates. These instructions describe how you can always have the entered content displayed.

Instruction

1. Open Excel with an empty workbook.
2. Enter the date *January 2024* in A1.

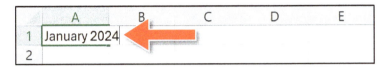

3. Confirm the entry using the *enter key* ⏎ and look at the result.

Result: Excel converts the date into the abbreviated notation *Jan-24*.

4. Enter *'January 2024* in A2. This time, place an apostrophe (') before the word *January*. Only enter a single apostrophe!

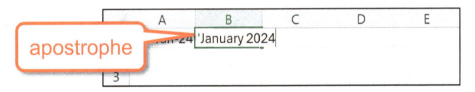

Advice: The apostrophe is inserted by pressing the *apostrophe key* ⌨.

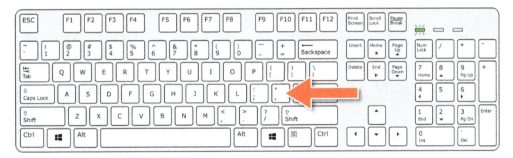

5. Confirm the entry using the *enter key* ⏎ and look at the result again.

Result: Excel does not shorten the date. The Apostrophe is not displayed. However, it is part of the content of the cell.

6. Close Excel without saving.

5   Using a key combination to change the zoom factor

These instructions describe how you can enlarge and reduce the size of a spreadsheet using the keyboard and mouse.

Instruction

1. Open the sample file: ***Chapter 05 - Vehicle invoice - B3***
   Attention: The file was downloaded from the internet. It is therefore possible that the file will be opened in **Protected View**. In this case, click on the Enable editing button in the yellow bar at the top of the program window.

2. Press and hold the ***control key*** ⬚Ctrl⬚ and turn the scroll wheel upward.

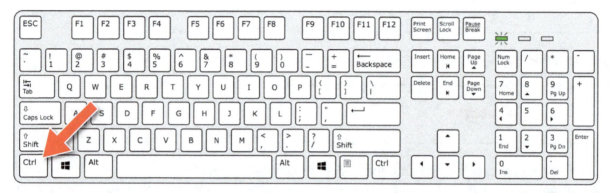

3. Look at the result.

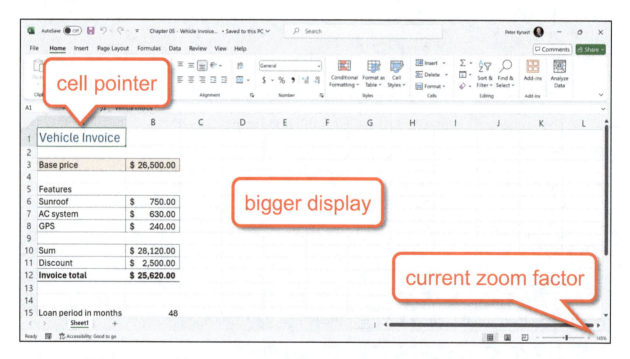

Result: The table is zoomed in (enlarged). The cell pointer (green frame) remains in your field of vision. Each time the scroll wheel ratches, the zoom setting changes by ***15 %***.

Advice: If you want to reduce the zoom factor, press and hold the ***control key*** ⬚Ctrl⬚ turn the scroll wheel backwards. The default setting for the zoom factor is 100 %. The last used zoom factor is saved in the Excel file and automatically reapplied the next time it is opened.

4. Close Excel without saving.

---

6   Scrolling horizontally in a table

Horizontal (sideways) scrolling (moving) was previously only possible with the horizontal scrollbar. Since the Excel 2016 version, you can also scroll sideways using the keyboard and the scroll wheel.

Instruction

1. Open the sample file: ***Chapter 06 - Consumption - B3***
2. Press and hold the ***control key*** `Ctrl` + ***shift key*** `⇧` and turn the scroll wheel back and forth.

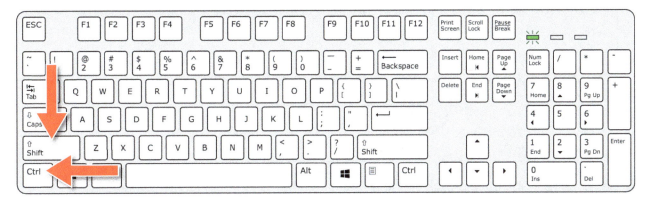

3. Look at the result.

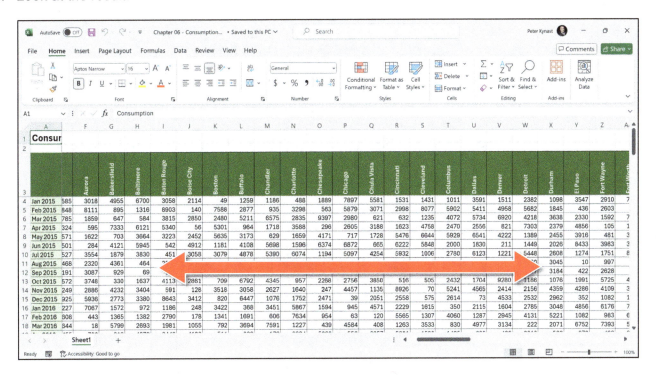

Result: The table is moved to the left and right (scrolled sideways).

Attention: Many companies use so-called remote desktop services. This technology is also known as a remote desktop environment. In this situation, side scrolling is not activated. Excel must be used as a local installation.

4. Close Excel without saving.

7 Copying formulas by double-clicking

These instructions describe how you can quickly copy a formula to any number of cells. This process is particularly useful for long lists.

Instruction

1. Open the sample file: ***Chapter 07 - Car sales - Start - B3***
2. Enter the formula ***=C2*1,08*** in D2 and confirm the entry with the ***enter key*** ⏎.

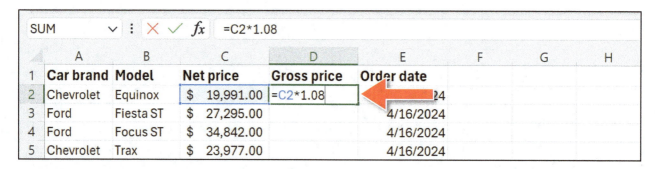

3. Select cell D2 and <u>double-click</u> on the fill handle in the bottom right of the cell pointer.

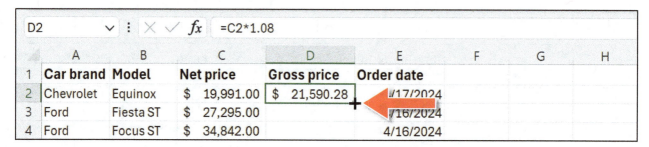

Result: As soon as you place the mouse on the fill handle (green square on the cell pointer), the mouse is displayed as a black cross **✛**. This cross is used to copy and fill cell contents.

4. Look at the result.

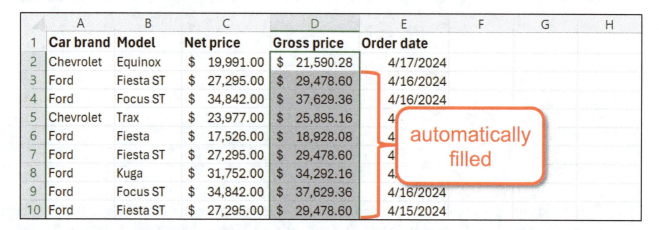

Result: The formula is automatically filled out to the end of the table. The cell references are automatically adjusted in the process.

5. Save the file and close Excel.

---

8 Displaying formulas

When opening external worksheets for the first time, you should first familiarize yourself with the structure and content. It is particularly important to know in which cells calculations take place. With the formula view, you can see all formulas directly and immediately have a good overview.

Instruction

1. Open the sample file: ***Chapter 08 - Price conversions - B3***

2. In the ***Formulas*** tab, click on the ***Show formulas*** button $\boxed{\sqrt{fx}\ \text{Show Formulas}}$ to display all formulas in the table.

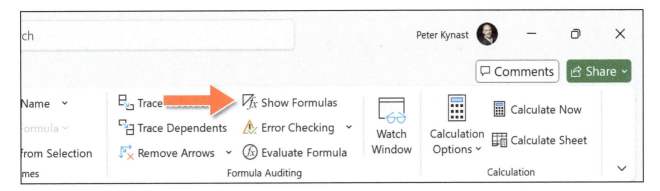

Or: Press the key combination ***control key*** $\boxed{\text{Ctrl}}$ + ***accent key*** $\boxed{\tilde{\ }}$.

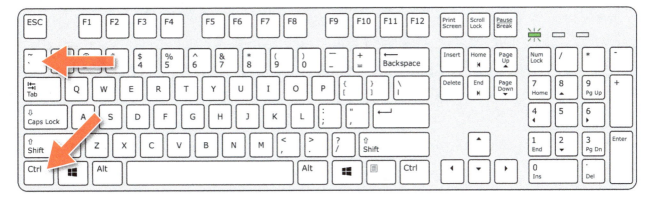

3. Look at the result.

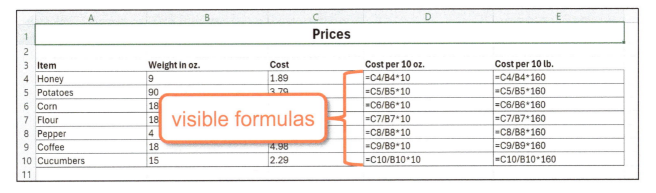

	A	B	C	D	E
1			Prices		
2					
3	Item	Weight in oz.	Cost	Cost per 10 oz.	Cost per 10 lb.
4	Honey	9	1.89	=C4/B4*10	=C4/B4*160
5	Potatoes	90	3.79	=C5/B5*10	=C5/B5*160
6	Corn	18		=C6/B6*10	=C6/B6*160
7	Flour	18		=C7/B7*10	=C7/B7*160
8	Pepper	4		=C8/B8*10	=C8/B8*160
9	Coffee	18	4.98	=C9/B9*10	=C9/B9*160
10	Cucumbers	15	2.29	=C10/B10*10	=C10/B10*160
11					

Result: All formulas in the table are visible. The columns are displayed in double width so that longer formulas can be read in full.

4. Select D4 and look at the result.

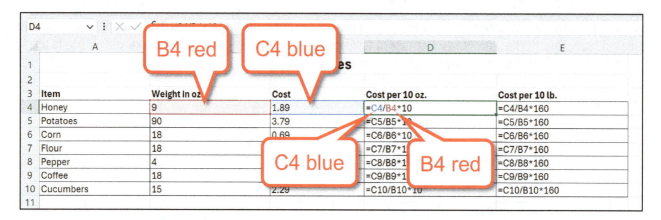

Result: The cell references in D4 are displayed in different colors. The corresponding cells are displayed in the same color. This makes it easier to assign the cell references to the cells.

5. Click the **Show formulas** button in the **Formulas** tab again to reactivate the normal view.

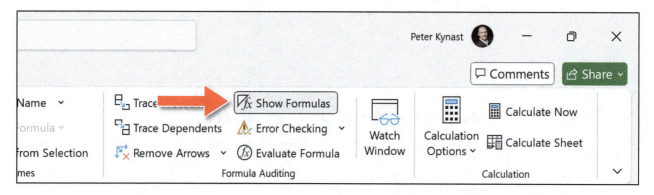

Result: Cells with formulas display the results of the formulas again. The columns are displayed at the original size again.

6. Close Excel without saving.

9   Navigating in large tables 1

Since Excel 2007, each Excel spreadsheet has 1048576 rows and 16384 columns. This guide describes how you can quickly reach the ends of the spreadsheet.

Instruction

1. Open Excel with an empty workbook.
2. Press the key combination **control key** Ctrl + **down arrow key** ↓.

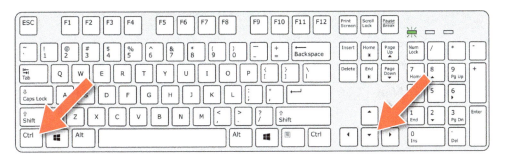

3. Look at the result. The cell pointer is placed in the last cell of column A.

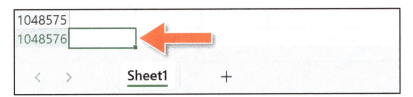

4. Press the key combination **control key** Ctrl + **right arrow key** → to move the cell pointer to the right in the last column. Look at the result.

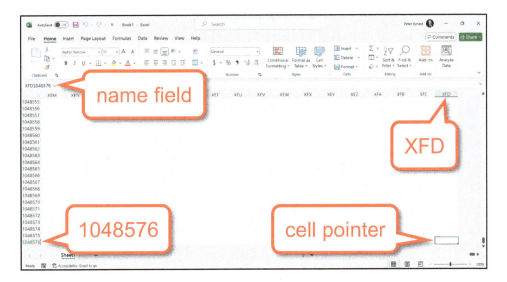

Result: The cell pointer is placed in the last cell of the sheet the bottom right.
Advice: The last cell of a table has the name XFD1048576. You can read the name of the cell in the name field.

5. Press the key combination **control key** Ctrl + **Home** Home to move the cell pointer to A1 or use the control key and the arrow keys again.
6. Close Excel without saving.

10   Navigating in large tables 2

These instructions describe how you can quickly reach the ends of a filled table.

Instruction

1. Open the sample file: *Chapter 10 - Computer - B3*
2. Select cell A1.

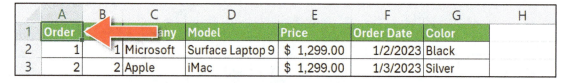

3. Press the key combination *control key* Ctrl + *down arrow key* ↓ to select the last cell with content in column A.

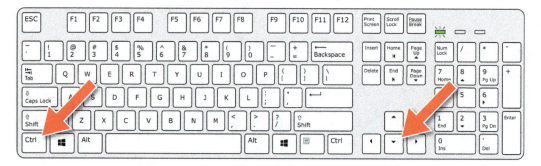

4. Look at the result.

Result: The cell pointer is placed in the last cell of this column that has content.
Attention: Empty cells interrupt a row. If a cell in a column or row is empty, the cell pointer remains in front of the empty cell.

5. Use key combination *control key* Ctrl + *arrow keys right*, →, *left* ← and *up* ↑ to navigate to the right, left and upper ends of the filled table.

6. Close Excel without saving.

11   Selecting in large tables 1

These instructions describe how you can quickly select large areas in tables.

Instruction

1. Open the sample file: ***Chapter 11 - Computer - B3***
2. Select cell A2.
3. Press the key combination ***control key*** Ctrl + ***shift key*** ⇧ + ***down arrow key*** ↓.

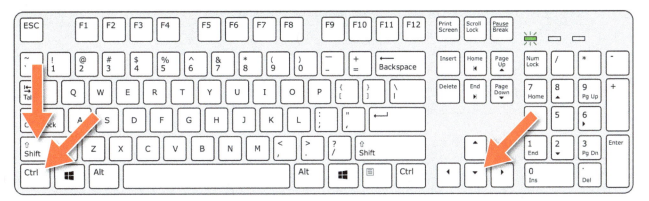

Advice: For key combinations consisting of 3 keys, press and hold the first two keys and then briefly press the third key. Then release the first two buttons again.

4. Look at the result.

126	125	123	Apple	iPad Air	$	599.00	11/11/2023	Grey	
127	126			iPad Air	$	599.00	11/13/2023	Grey	
128									

Result: The range from A2 to the last cell in this column with content (A127) is selected.

5. Press the key combination ***shift key*** ⇧ + ***right arrow key*** → to select column B as well.

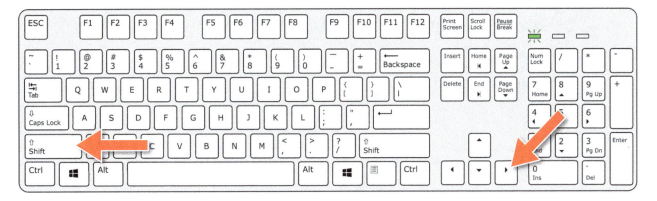

6. Look at the result. The selection has been extended to column B.

126	125	123	Apple	iPad Air	$	599.00	11/11/2023	Grey	
127	126	124		d Air	$	599.00	11/13/2023	Grey	
128									

7. Close Excel without saving.

12   Selecting in large tables 2

These instructions describe how you can select a table of any size.

Instruction

1. Open the sample file: **_Chapter 12 - Computer - B3_**
2. Place the cell pointer on <u>any</u> cell within the cell range A1 to G127.

3. Press the key combination **_control key_** `Ctrl` + `A` to select the whole table.

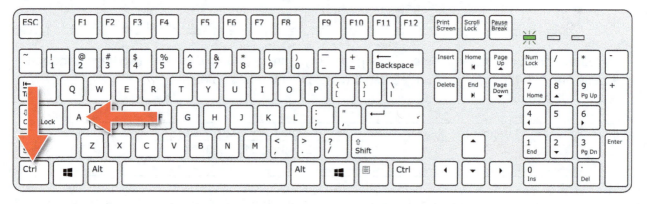

4. Look at the result.

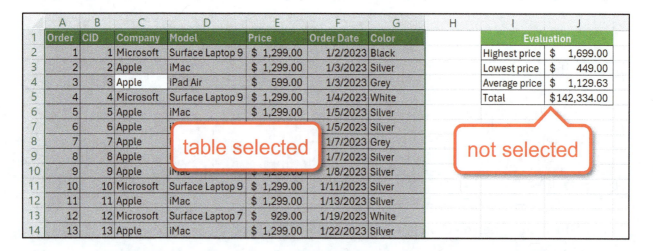

Result: The table is recognized as a connected data range and is fully selected. The previously selected cell is displayed transparently. It is the active cell. The second table is not selected.
Attention: Empty columns and rows interrupt a data area. The selection is only extended up to the empty columns and rows.

5. Close Excel without saving.

13 Displaying negative values in red

These instructions describe how you can automatically display negative values in red.

Instruction

1. Open the sample file: ***Chapter 13 - Checking account - Start - B3***
2. Select the cell range C4 to D16.
3. Click on the arrow ⬘ in the **Number** group to open the **Format Cells** dialog box.

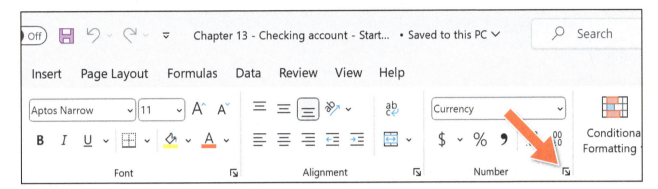

4. Click on the **Currency** category and in this category on the second list item in the **Negative numbers** field to activate red numbers for negative values.

5. Click on the **OK** button and look at the result.

3	Date	Posting text	Amount	Balance
4	1/1/2024	Starting balance		$512.36
5	1/1/2024	Rent	$420.00	$92.36
6	1/2/2024	Car insurance	$54.22	$38.14
7	1/2/2024	ATM	$100.00	$61.86
8	1/2/2024	Wage, salary	$1,547.00	$1,485.14

negative values in red

Result: Negative values are displayed in red. The positive values remain unchanged.

Advice: You also have the option of displaying negative values in red in the **Number** category.

6. Save the file and close Excel.

14   Revising lists using flash fill

These instruction describe how to combine the contents of 2 cells in another column.

Instruction

1. Open the sample file: *Chapter 14 - Roster - Start - B3*
2. Enter the name *John Long* in C2 and confirm the entry.

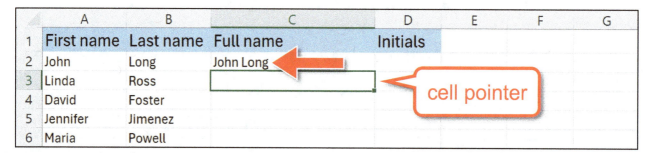

3. In the **Home** tab, click on the *Fill* button and then on *Flash Fill*. Make sure that the cell pointer is positioned on cell C3.

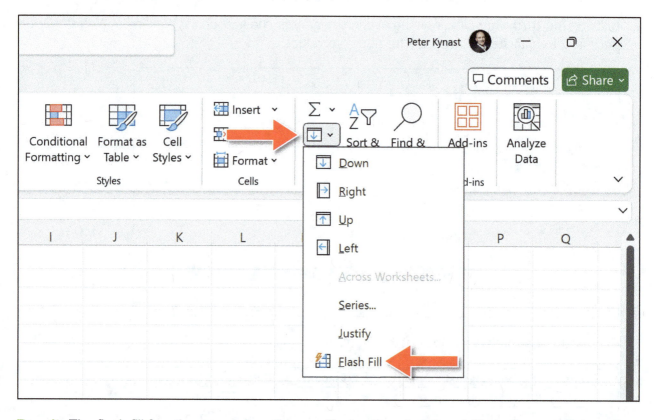

Result: The flash fill function recognizes the specified pattern in C2 and fills in the rest of the column automatically.

Attention: The flash fill function does not work dynamically! If you change names in column A or B, the values in column C are <u>not</u> automatically adjusted. You must repeat the process. For the values to be filled correctly, you must delete the wrong values in the filled column and click on **Flash Fill** again. If a cell is already filled and it does not match the pattern of the other cells, flash fill will not work.

4. Look at the result.

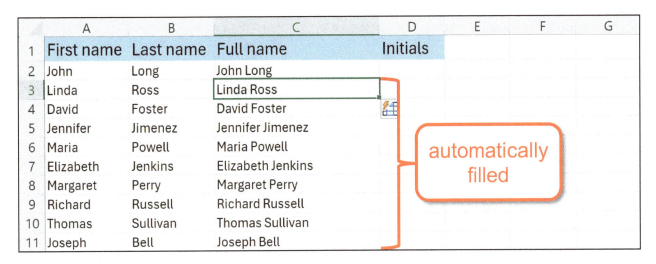

Result: The following names are automatically combined.

5. Enter the initials of John Long (JL) in cell D2.

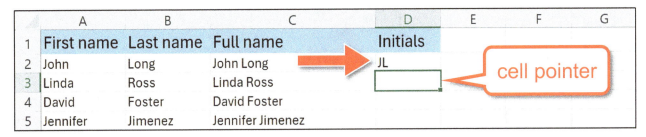

6. Click on the **Fill → Flash Fill** button again to fill in the following cells with the initials. Look at the result.

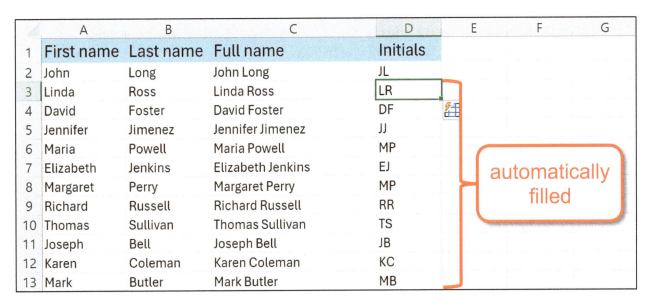

Result: The initials are also filled in automatically.

Advice: The flash fill function can recognize a wide variety of patterns. Try out other automatic data completions.

7. Save the file and close Excel.

15   Moving cells between other cells

These instructions describe how you can move cells <u>between</u> other cells.

Instruction

1. Open the sample file: ***Chapter 15 - Speed conversions - Start - B3***
2. Select the range C3 to C9.
   Advice: The ***kph*** column should be placed between the columns ***Traffic area*** and ***mph***.
3. Point to the edge of the cell pointer with the mouse. Do <u>not</u> point to the fill handle.

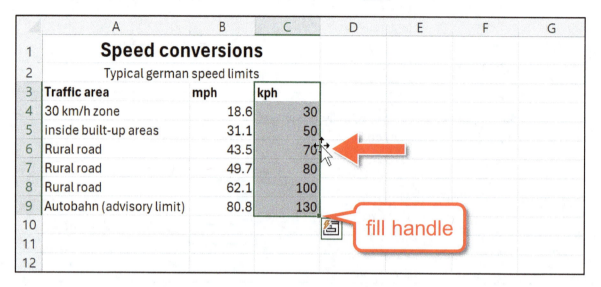

Result: The mouse pointer is displayed as a mouse with 4 arrows ![mouse pointer icon]. This mouse pointer symbolizes the moving of cells.
Advice: The fill handle is used to copy formulas and formats and cannot be used to move cells. When you point to the fill handle, the mouse pointer is displayed as a black cross **+**.

4. Click on the edge and hold down the mouse button.
5. Press the ***shift key*** ⇧ and keep the button pressed.

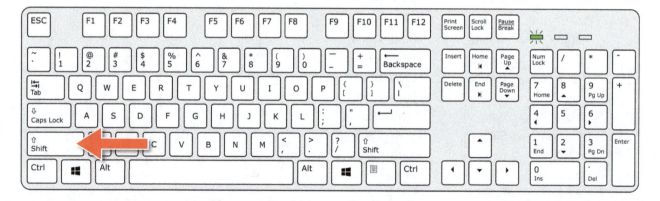

6. Drag the column to the left between the *Traffic area* and *mph* columns (A and B). Pay attention to the green bar and the tooltip. Both show the target area.

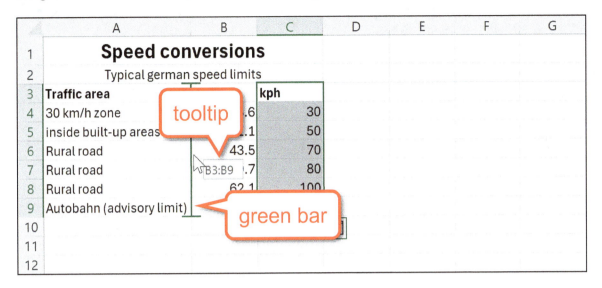

7. First release the mouse button and <u>then</u> the **shift key** ⬆. Look at the result.

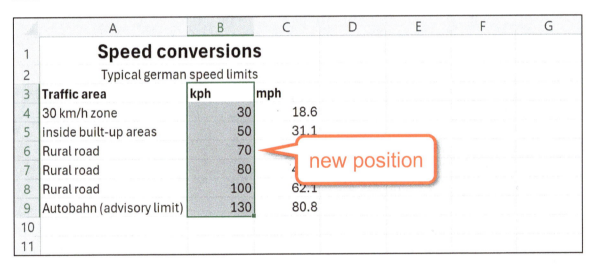

Result: The kph column is moved <u>between</u> the *Traffic area* and the *mph* columns. The *mph* column is moved to the right.

Attention: If you release the Shift button first, you will cause the cells to be overwritten. You will receive a warning. Click on the *Cancel* button and repeat the process.

Advice: Rows can also be moved between other rows in the same way. <u>Always pay attention to the green bar</u>. It shows you at which position you are inserting the rows. When moving rows, the bar must be displayed horizontally.

8. Save the file and close Excel.

16   Copying values to the cell below 1

These instructions describe how to copy values to the cell below using a key combination. This process is useful if values are often repeated in lists.

Instruction

1. Open the sample file: ***Chapter 16 - Logbook - Start - B3***
2. Select cell A14.

12	1/5/2024 Company	Client Jackson	10502
13	1/5/2024 Client Jackson	Company	10543
14			
15			
16			

Advice: A new customer visit should be entered in row 14. As in row 13, this is a trip on 1/5/2024.

3. Press the key combination ***control key*** Ctrl + D .

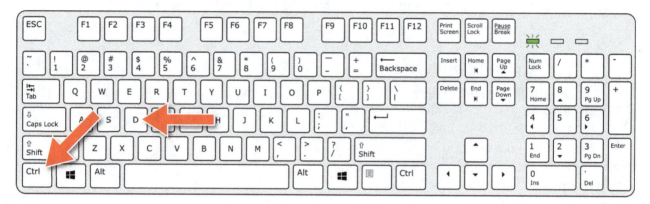

4. Look at the result.

12	1/5/2024 Company	Client Jackson	10502
13	1/5/2024 Client Jackson	Company	10543
14	1/5/2024		
15			
16			

Result: The date of the cell above is copied ***downwards***.

Advice: If you want to copy the content of the left-hand cell to the adjacent cell on the right, press the key combination ***control key*** Ctrl + R (R as in ***right***).

5. Save the file and close Excel.

17   Copying values to the cell below 2

Each cell has an invisible list box. When this list box is opened, it displays the contents of the cells directly above it. In this way, previous content can be copied quickly and typing can be avoided.

Instruction

1. Open the sample file: ***Chapter 17 - Orders - Start - B3***
2. Select C11 and press the key combination ⎡Alt⎤ + ***down arrow key*** ⎡↓⎤.

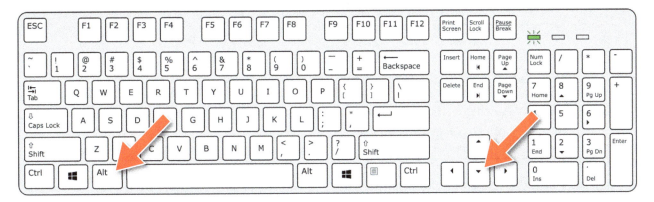

Result: The list box of the cell is opened. It contains the texts that were entered in the cells above it.

3. Use the arrow keys ⎡↑⎤ and ⎡↓⎤ to select the desired list item.

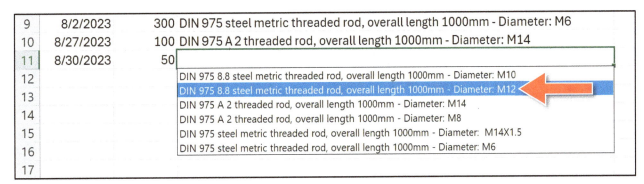

4. Confirm your selection with the ***enter key*** ⎡↵⎤.

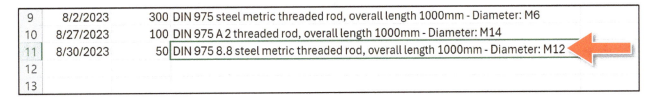

Result: The text is entered in the cell.

5. Save the file and close Excel.

18 Smart tables 1

These instructions describe how to convert a data range into a smart table. Smart tables offer automatisms that are not available in normal tables, e.g. result rows, automatic filling, quick filters or design templates.

Instruction

1. Open the sample file: **_Chapter 18 - Furniture - Start - B3_**
2. Click on any cell in the range A1 to F40 to select this range.

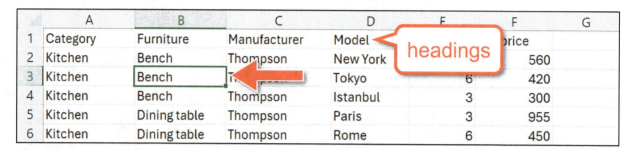

Advice: For Excel to be able to assign a smart table, the cell pointer must be within the data range that is to be converted. Please also note that the first row of the data range contains headers.

3. Click on the **_Table_** button in the **_Insert_** tab to open the **_Create Table_** dialog box.

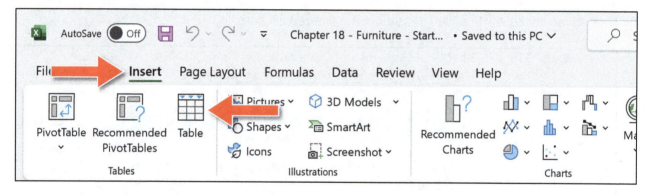

Or: Click on the **_Format as table_** button in the **_Home_** tab and select any design from the list.

4. Check the data range and the header setting and confirm the entry with the **_OK_** button.

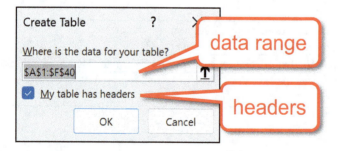

5. Look at the result.

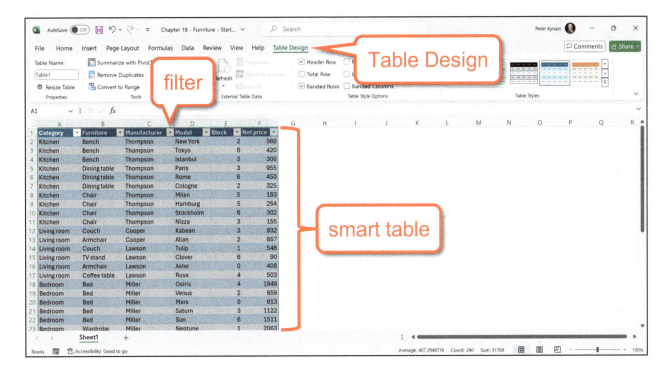

Result: The data range is converted into a smart table. Filter buttons are displayed in the header row. The rows of the table are displayed with a color change from light blue to white. This display is helpful for large tables to make it easier to distinguish the rows by eye. The area is highlighted. If the intelligent table is selected or the cell pointer is within the intelligent table, the **Table Design** tab is also displayed. This tab contains tools for the smart table.

6. Click on a cell <u>outside</u> the smart table and look at the result.

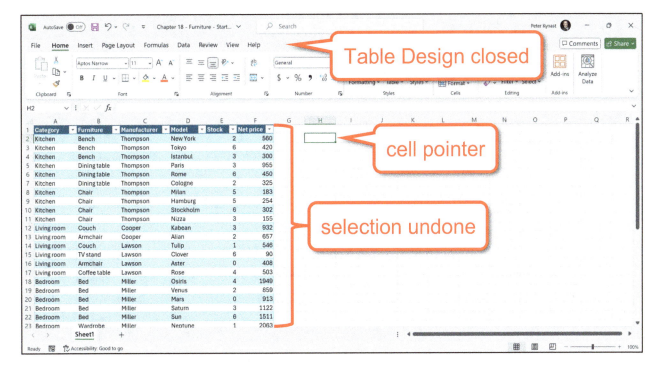

Result: The **Table Design** tab is closed and is no longer displayed. The table is no longer selected.

7. Click on any cell within the intelligent table to make the **Table Design** tab visible again.

8. Click on the **Table Design** tab to activate this tab.

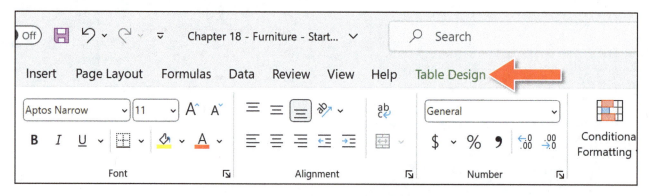

Attention: The tab is only displayed if the cell pointer is in the smart table or the smart table is selected. If the cell pointer is outside the smart table, this tab is <u>not</u> displayed.

9. In the **Table Design** tab, activate the **Total Row** checkbox to show the total row of the smart table.

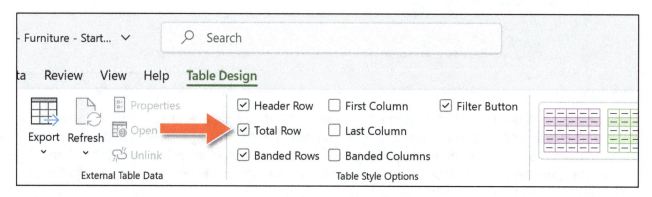

10. Look at the result.

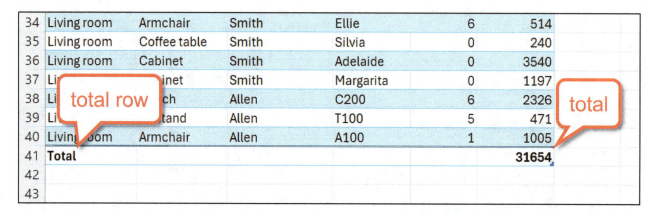

Result: The total row is displayed in row 41. The sum of column F is calculated in F41.

Advice: When the total row is displayed, a total is displayed in the last column by default. As column F contains numbers, the sum is calculated. If there are texts in the last column of the smart table, Excel would output the number of words.

11. Save the file and close Excel.

19   Smart tables 2

These instructions describe how you can display additional results in the total row of a smart table.

Instruction

1. Open the sample file: ***Chapter 19 - Furniture - Intermediate result 1 - B3***
2. Select cell F41 and click on the arrow next to the cell.

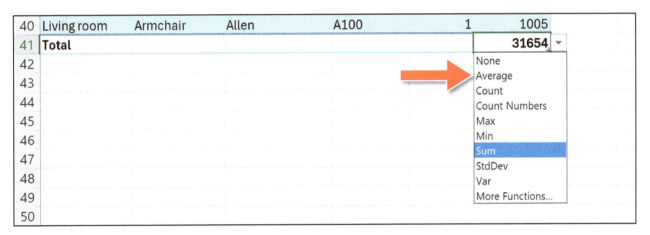

Result: A list box with various calculation methods is displayed.

Advice: While the standard name of the

3. Click on the **Average** function in the list to calculate the average value in F41.

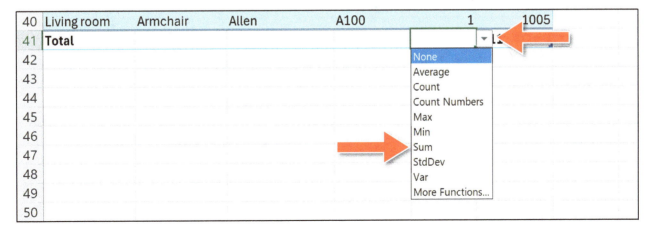

4. Select E41 and open the list box for this cell. Set the **Sum** function.

5. Save the file and close Excel.

20   Smart tables 3

These instructions describe how you can activate simple filters in smart tables.

Instruction

1. Open the sample file: ***Chapter 20 - Furniture - Intermediate result 2 - B3***
2. Click on the arrow next to the ***Manufacturer*** heading to open the filter settings.

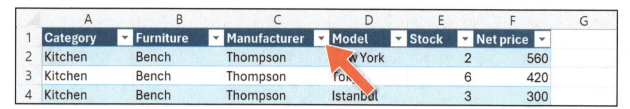

3. First click on the ***(Select All)*** list item to remove all check marks. Then click on the manufacturer ***Lawson*** to reactivate this list item.

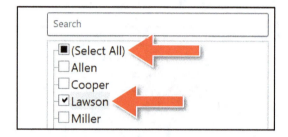

4. Click on the ***OK*** button and look at the result.

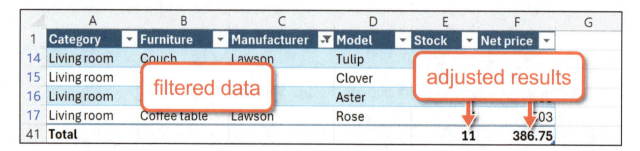

Result: The data is filtered. Only furniture from the manufacturer Lehmann is displayed. The results are adapted to the current filter settings. The row numbers are displayed in blue. This highlighting indicates the active filter.

5. Next to the Manufacturer heading, click on the filter symbol and then on ***Clear Filter From "Manufacturer"*** to remove the filter again.

Advice: You can also activate filters in several columns at the same time.
6. Close Excel without saving.

---

21   Smart tables 4

These instruction describe how you can quickly activate filters in the smart table.

Instruction

1. Open the sample file: ***Chapter 21 - Furniture - Intermediate result 3 - B3***
2. Place the cell pointer in the smart table to select it.
3. Click on the ***Insert Slicer*** button in the ***Table Design*** tab.

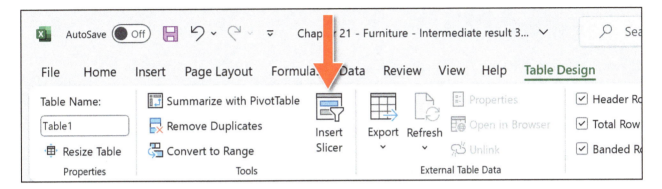

Result: The ***Insert Slicers*** dialog box appears.

4. Activate the checkbox in the ***Manufacturer*** column.

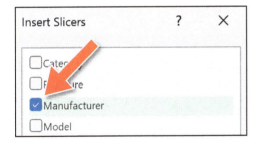

5. Click on the ***OK*** button and look at the result.

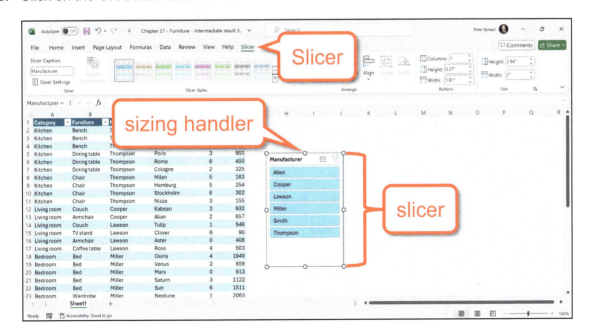

Result: The slicer window is placed in the center of the screen. The window is selected. This is made clear by the sizing handlers, which only appear while the slicer is selected. As the window is selected, the *Slicer* tab is also visible.

6. Click on the manufacturer *Cooper* in the *Slicer* window to activate this filter.

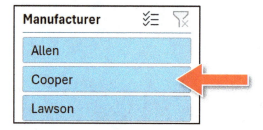

7. Look at the result.

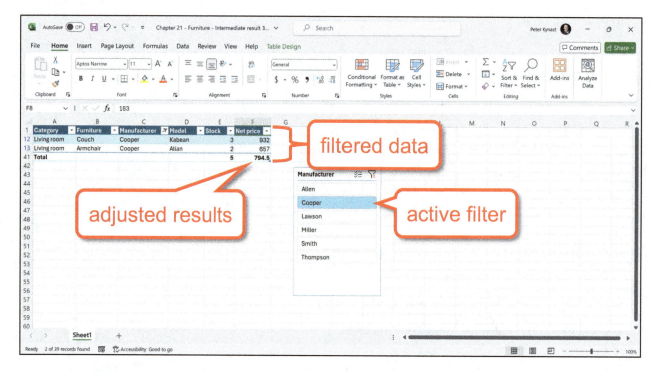

Result: The filter is applied. In the *Slicer* window, the active *Cooper* filter is highlighted in blue.

8. Click on the *Multi-Select* button in the *Slicer* window.

Advice: By activating Multi-Select, several filters can be set at the same time.

9. Click on the manufacturer **Lawson** in the **Slicer** to add this filter <u>additionally</u>.

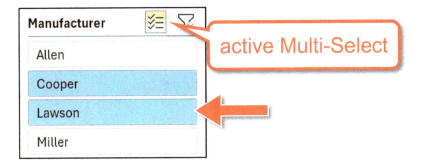

Result: The smart table only shows the data for **Cooper** and **Lawson**.

10. Click on the **Clear Filter** and **Multi-Select** buttons to remove the filter and the multiple selection.

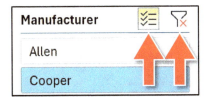

11. Click on the title area of the **Slicer** window and drag it up to row 1, leaving columns G and H empty. Data will be inserted here later.

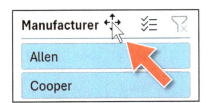

12. Look at the result.

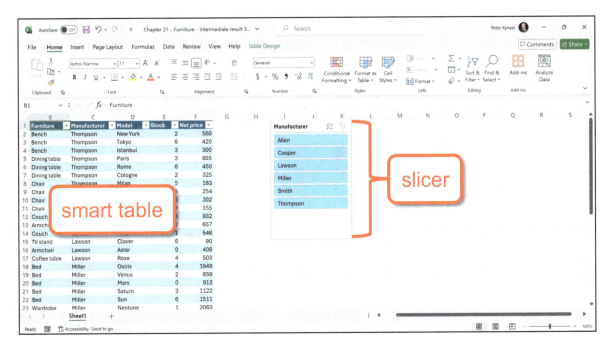

13. Save the file and close Excel.

22   Smart tables 5

These instructions describe how to add a column with formulas to the smart table.

Instruction

1. Open the sample file: *Chapter 22 - Furniture - Intermediate result 4 - B3*
2. Enter the heading *Gross price* in cell G1.

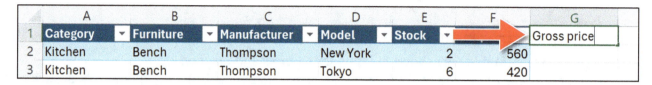

3. Press the *enter key* ↵ and look at the result.

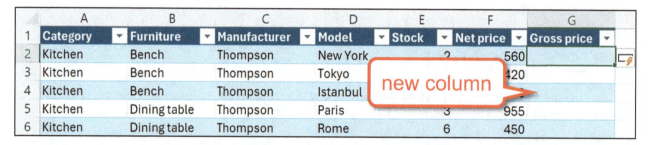

Result: Column G is automatically added to the smart table. It adopts the same formats.

4. Enter the formula *=F2*1.08* in G2 to calculate the gross price.

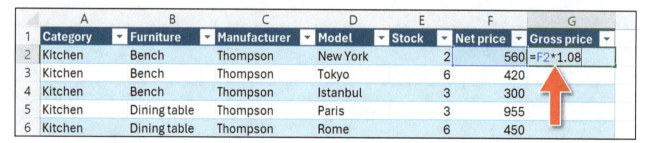

5. Confirm the entry with the *enter key* ↵ and look at the result.

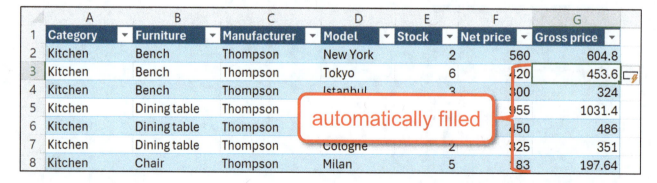

Result: The cells below in column G are filled in automatically. The formats are adjusted in the process.

6. Save the file and close Excel.

23   Smart tables 6

These instructions describe how to add a new row to the smart table.

Instruction

1. Open the sample file: ***Chapter 23 - Furniture - Intermediate result 5 - B3***
2. Press the key combination ***control key*** Ctrl + End to move the cell pointer to the last cell in the table (G41).

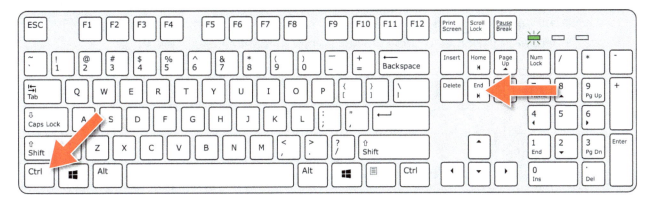

3. Look at the result.

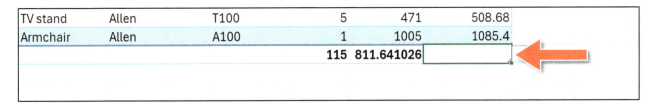

TV stand	Allen	T100	5	471	508.68
Armchair	Allen	A100	1	1005	1085.4
			115	811.641026	

4. Press the key combination ***control key*** Ctrl + ***equal sign key*** = to add a new row to the smart table.

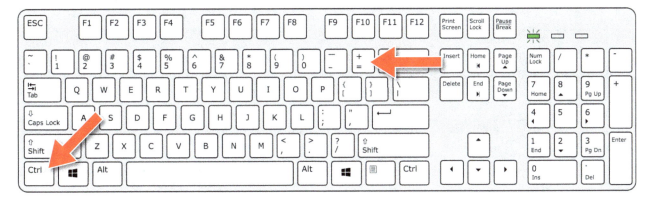

5. Look at the result.

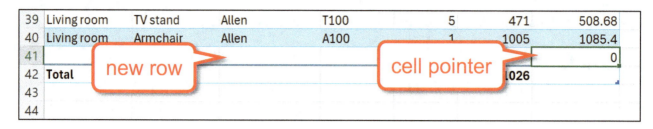

Result: A new row is added to the intelligent table. The result row is moved down one row. The new row is placed <u>between</u> row 40 and the total row. The cell pointer is positioned on cell G41.

6. Press the **Home key** `Home` to place the cell pointer in the first cell of row 41.

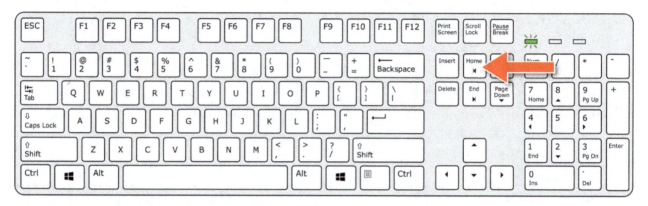

7. Look at the result.

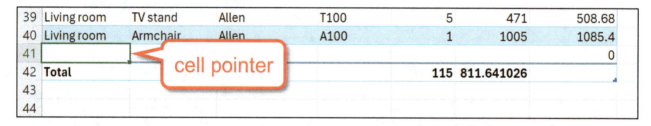

8. Enter the following data in the new row (41). Pay attention to the gross price in cell G41. It will be calculated automatically as soon as you have entered the net price in cell 41 and confirmed the entry. You can also use the keyboard shortcut **control key** `Ctrl` + `D` to fill the cells faster.

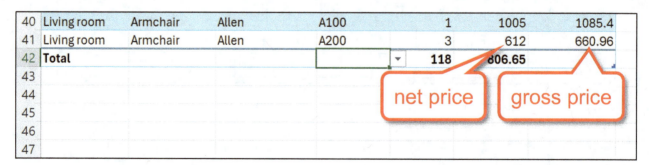

Advice: The key combination **control key** `Ctrl` + `D` automatically repeats the value from the cell above.

9. Save the file and close Excel.

24   Inserting a chart in a new sheet

These instructions describe how to insert a chart as a new sheet using a keyboard shortcut.

Instruction

1. Open the sample file: ***Chapter 24 - Museums - Start - B3***
2. Select the cell range A4 to D8.

   Or: Click in the area from A4 to D8 and press the key combination ***control key*** Ctrl + A to select the area.

3. Press the ***function key*** F11 to insert a chart in a new sheet tab.

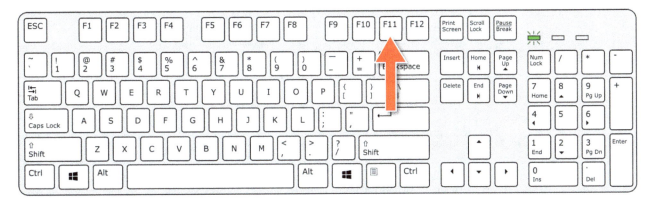

4. Look at the result.

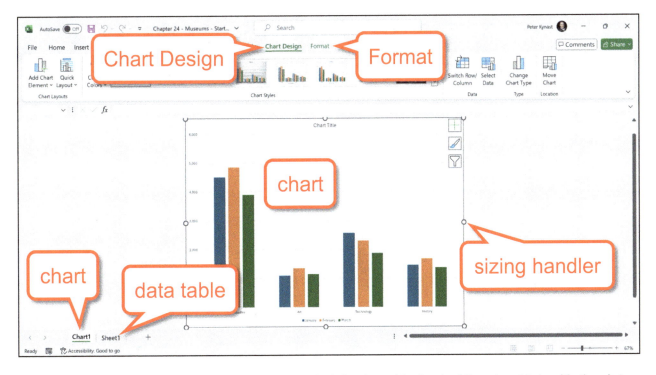

Result: The chart is inserted as a <u>new</u> sheet tab. It is placed in front of the sheet tab with the data (Table1) and is labeled ***Chart1***. The chart is selected. For this reason, the ***Chart Design*** and ***Format*** tabs are displayed. You can recognize the selection by the sizing handlers. As soon as you deselect the chart, these two additional tabs are hidden again.

5. Save the file and close Excel.

25   Inserting a chart into the current sheet

These instructions describe how you can insert a chart as an object in a spreadsheet using a key combination.

Instruction

1. Open the sample file: ***Chapter 25 - Revenue - Start - B3***
2. Select the cell range A3 to B8.
3. Press the key combination ⟨Alt⟩ + ⟨F1⟩ to insert a chart.

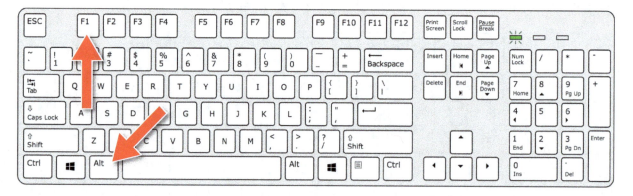

Advice: The following applies to button combinations: Hold down the first button and briefly press the second button. Then release the first button again.

4. Look at the result.

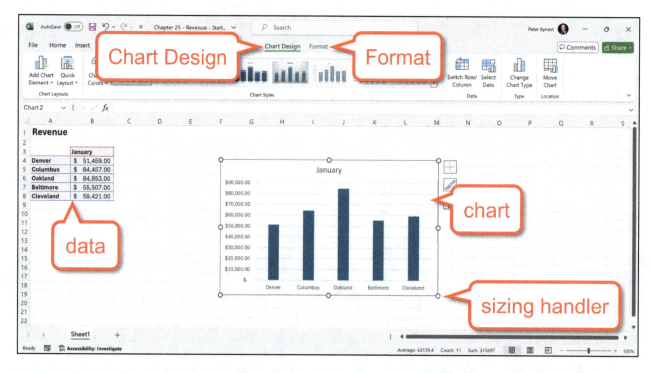

Result: The chart is inserted. Axis labels, a heading and a standard chart style template are assigned automatically. The ***Chart Design*** and ***Format*** tabs are displayed. The ***Chart Design*** tab is currently active. The two tabs contain tools and designs for charts. However, they are only visible if the chart is selected. You can recognize a selected chart by the 8 sizing handlers around it.

5. Save the file and close Excel.

© 2024 - www.ityco.com

26   Adjusting objects to cell positions

These instructions describe how you can anchor objects (charts, shapes, photos or buttons) that are in a spreadsheet to a precise cell position.

Instruction

1. Open the sample file: ***Chapter 26 - Revenue - Intermediate result - B3***
2. Press and hold the Alt key.

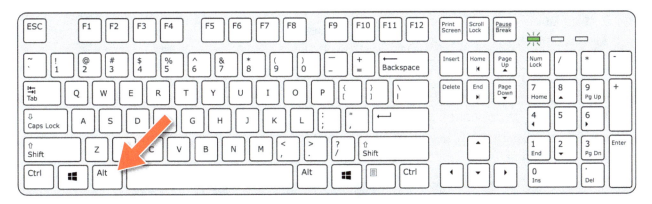

3. In the chart, click on the left or right area next to the heading and drag it to cell D3. The top left-hand corner of the chart should be placed exactly on cell D3.

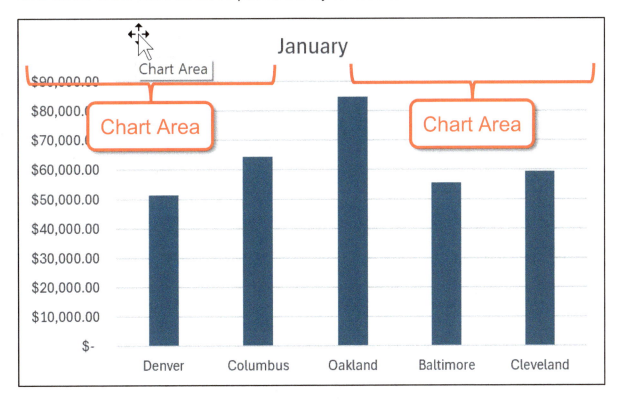

Advice: To move a chart, you must click on the so-called chart area. You can also recognize the chart area by the tooltip when you point to the area with the mouse. The chart area does not contain any data.

Attention: If you click on a different position in the chart, e.g. on the columns or the labels, you will move the elements within the chart. In this case, click on the ***Undo*** button and repeat the process.

4. Look at the result.

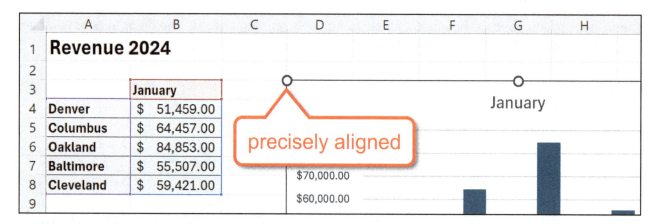

Result: Holding down the Alt key aligns the position of the chart with the borders of the cells. In this way, it can be positioned precisely.

5. Continue to keep the Alt key pressed and point the mouse to the sizing handler at the bottom center of the chart.

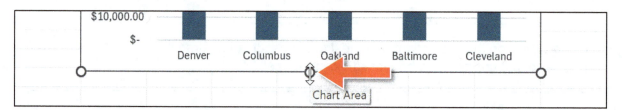

6. Drag the mouse to the cell border between rows 19 and 20 to enlarge it exactly to this grid line.

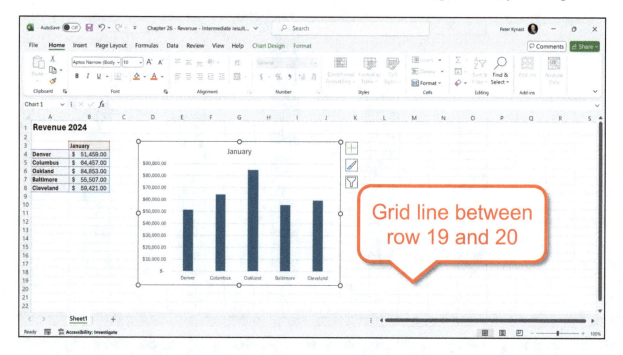

Result: By holding down the Alt key the chart snaps into place when dragged and can therefore be precisely aligned with the cell borders.

7. Release the Alt key again.

8. Save the file and close Excel.

---

27 Extending the data range of a chart 1

These instruction describe how you can quickly extend the data area of a chart.

Instruction

1. Open the sample file: *Chapter 27 - Business trips - Start - B3*
2. Click on the chart to select it.
   Result: The data range of the diagram A5 to A7 and B4 to B7 is highlighted.
3. Place the mouse pointer on the bottom right corner of the data area.

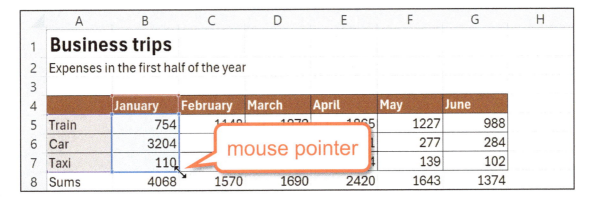

Result: The mouse pointer is displayed as a diagonal double arrow ↖.

4. Hold down the left mouse button and drag the mouse to the right to add the month of *February* to the data area.

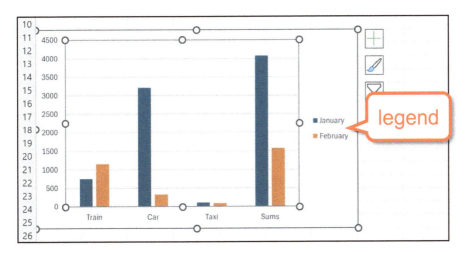

5. Look at the result.

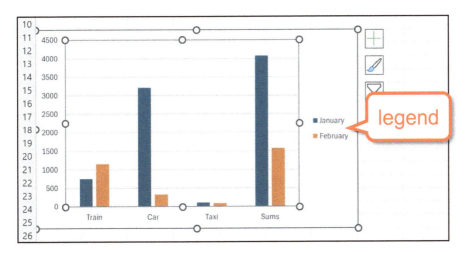

Result: The month of February is included in the chart. The legend shows 2 months.

6. Save the file and close Excel.

28   Extending the data range of a chart 2

These instructions describe how you can extend the data range of a diagram. In this example, we are dealing with a data range that is not adjacent to the existing range.

Instruction

1. Open the sample file: ***Chapter 28 - Breads - Start - B3***
2. Select the cell range D4 to D9.
   Advice: The months January and March are to be compared. March is therefore added to the chart.
3. Click on the ***Copy*** button in the ***Home*** tab to copy the data.

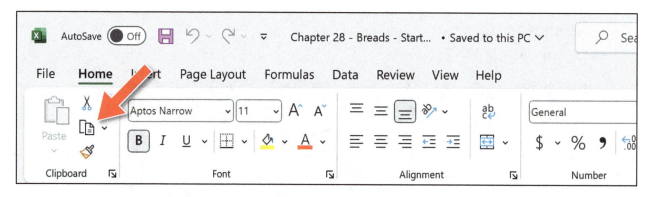

Or: Press the key combination ***control key*** `Ctrl` + `C`.

4. Click anywhere on the chart to select it.
5. Click on the ***Paste*** button to insert the data into the chart.

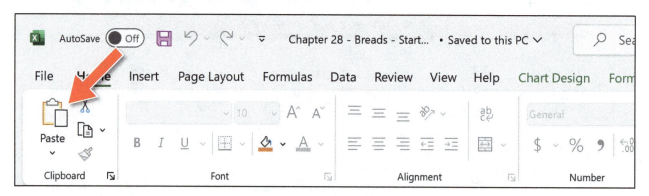

Or: Press the key combination ***control key*** `Ctrl` + `V`.

6. Look at the result. The month of March is added to the chart.

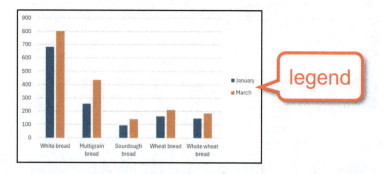

7. Save the file and close Excel.

29   Searching in values

By default, Excel's search function searches for fixed values and for values used <u>within</u> formulas. Results from formulas that display the value you are looking for are <u>not</u> found and can therefore be easily overlooked.

Instruction

1. Open the sample file: **Chapter 29 - Bicycles - B3**
2. Press the key combination **control key** Ctrl + F to open the **Find and Replace** dialog box.

Or: Click on the **Find & Select → Find** button in the **home** tab.

3. Enter the value **394** in the search field and confirm the entry with the **enter key** ↵ or click on the **Find Next** button.

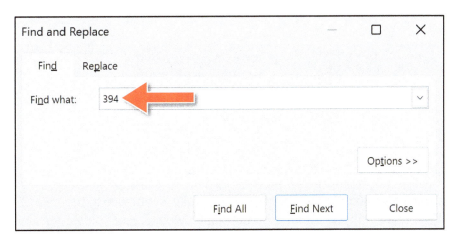

4. Look at the result.

Result: Although the value is present in cell P16, it is <u>not</u> found by the search.
Attention: If the file is still opened in the **Protected View**, the value 394 is found. By default, the protected view searches for <u>values</u> and not <u>formulas</u>.

5. Confirm the message with the *OK* button. The search window is displayed again.
6. Click on the *Options* button to display the other search options.

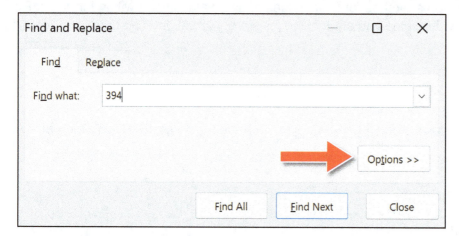

7. In the Search in field, select the *Values* entry and confirm your entry with *enter key* ⏎ or the *Find Next* button.

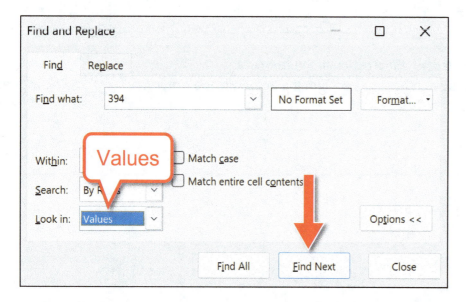

Advice: By default, Excel searches for texts and numbers that have been entered in the cells. Excel also searches for values that are used <u>within</u> formulas. By default, however, Excel does <u>not</u> search for the results of formulas.

8. Look at the result.

35	23	36	68	22
55	66	21	95	23
584	512	394		610
50	77	38	47	63
33	93	32	102	84

Result: The value is found in cell P16.
Attention: If you have selected a data range before accessing the search function, only the selected area will be searched.

9. Close Excel without saving.

30   Partially solving formulas

These instructions describe how you can solve parts of a formula. In this way, you can understand formulas step by step. This is particularly helpful for complex formulas.

Instruction

1. Open the sample file: ***Chapter 30 - Commissions - B3***
2. <u>Double-click</u> on cell C4 to activate the edit mode for this cell.
3. Select the first cell reference of B4 in the formula.

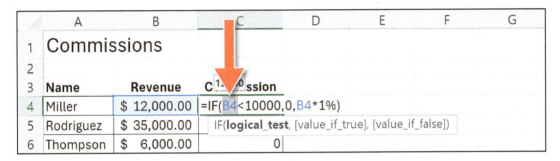

	A	B	C	D	E	F	G
1	Commissions						
2							
3	Name	Revenue	Commission				
4	Miller	$ 12,000.00	=IF(B4<10000,0,B4*1%)				
5	Rodriguez	$ 35,000.00	IF(**logical_test**, [value_if_true], [value_if_false])				
6	Thompson	$ 6,000.00	0				

4. Press the ***function key*** F9 to solve this part of the formula. Look at the result.

	A	B	C	D	E	F	G
1	Commissions						
2							
3	Name	Revenue	Commission				
4	Miller	$ 12,000.00	=IF(12000<10000,0,B4*1%)				
5	Rodriguez	$ 35,000.00	IF(**logical_test**, [value_if_true], [value_if_false])				

Result: The content of B4 (12000) is used for the cell reference.

5. Select the check ***12000<10000***.

	A	B	C	D
2				
3	Name	Revenue	Commi FALSE	
4	Miller	$ 12,000.00	=IF(12000<10000,0,B4*1%)	
5	Rodriguez	$ 35,000.00	IF(**logical_test**, [value_if_true], [value_if_false])	

6. Press the ***function key*** F9 again and look at the result.

	A	B	C
3	Name	Revenue	Commission
4	Miller	$ 12,000.00	=IF(FALSE,0,B4*1%)
5	Rodriguez	$ 35,000.00	IF(**logical_test**, [value_if_true], [value_if_false])
6	Thompson	$ 6,000.00	0

Result: The result of the check is displayed. The result is ***FALSE*** because 12000 is not less than 10000.

Attention: Do <u>not</u> press the ***enter key*** ↵. This would apply the changes to the formula.

7. Press the ***escape key*** Esc to exit edit mode without making any changes.
8. Close Excel without saving.

31   Freezing panes 1

These instructions describe how you can freeze rows. Frozen rows are always visible when scrolling up and down. This technique is therefore useful for long tables.

Instruction

1. Open the sample file: ***Chapter 31 - Cakes - Start - B3***
2. Select cell A5.

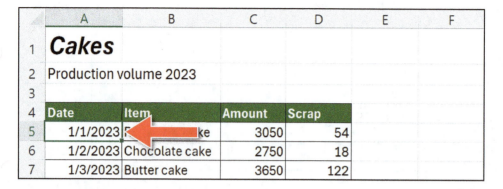

Advice: The position of the cell pointer is decisive for freezing. All rows above the cell pointer are frozen. They contain the headings and should always be visible when scrolling.

3. Click on the **View** tab.

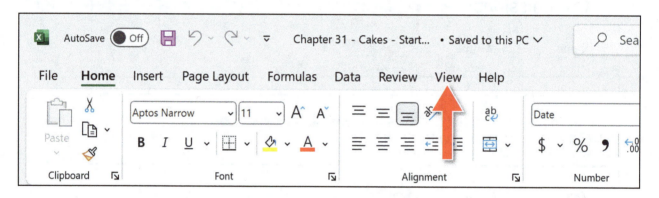

4. Click on the ***Freeze Panes*** button ⊞ to open the list box for this button.

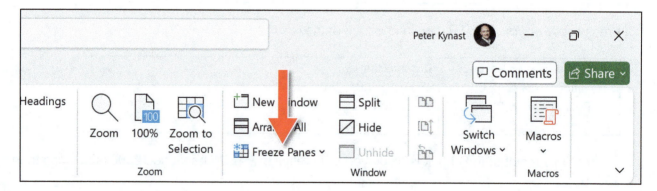

© 2024 - www.ityco.com

5. Click on the *Freeze Panes* list item to activate it.

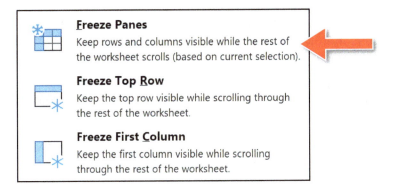

6. Scroll up and down with the mouse or the scroll bar and look at the result.

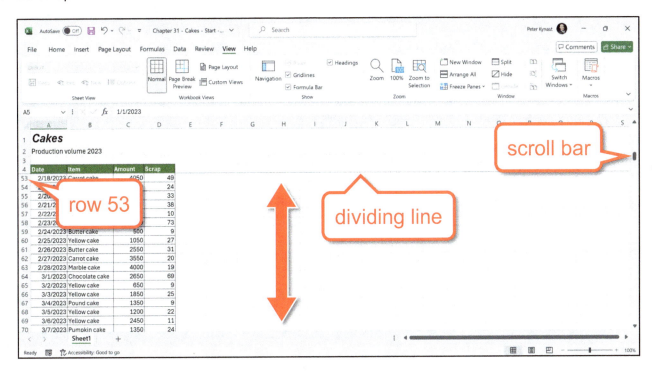

Result: The first 4 rows are frozen. This means that they are always visible when scrolling. There is a dividing line below row 4. It indicates the frozen rows.

Advice: This example is a long table. The first rows have therefore been frozen. In this way, the headings always remain in view. In wide tables, it often makes sense to freeze columns. Always pay attention to the position of the cell pointer. The following rule applies: All columns to the left of the cell pointer and all rows above the cell pointer are frozen. For example, if you want to fix column A and rows 1 to 4, the cell pointer must first be placed in cell B5. The frozen panes are saved with the file. If you want to unfreeze the panes, click the *Freeze Panes* button in the *View* tab again and then click *Unfreeze Panes*. Many users leave the rows and columns permanently frozen (pinned) in their tables.

7. Save the file and close Excel.

32 Freezing panes 2

These instructions describe how you can freeze rows and columns. Frozen columns always remain visible when scrolling sideways. This technique is therefore useful in wide tables.

Instruction

1. Open the sample file: ***Chapter 32 - Office supplies - Start - B3***
2. Select cell B4.

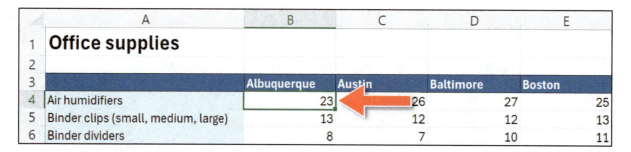

Advice: Column A and rows 1 to 3 should be frozen. Therefore, the cell pointer must be placed in cell B4 in this situation. The following rule applies: All columns to the left of the cell pointer and all rows above the cell pointer are frozen.

3. In the ***View*** tab, click on the ***Freeze Panes → Freeze Panes*** button to freeze the cells.
4. Scroll down and to the right. Look at the result.

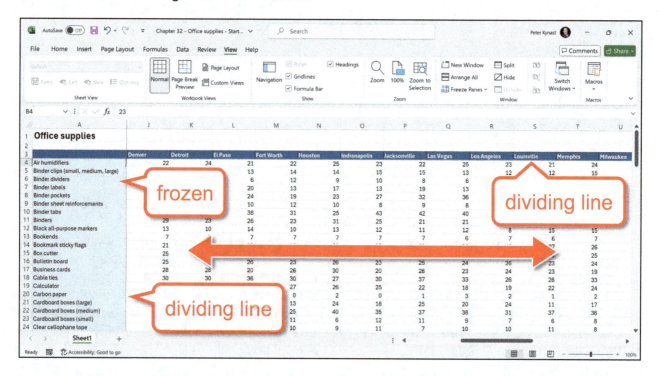

Result: Column A always remains visible when scrolling sideways. Dividing lines are displayed to the right of column A and below row 3. They indicate the frozen area. However, the horizontal dividing line below row 3 is not clearly visible due to the dark fill color in row 3.

5. Scroll up and down the table. Rows 1 to 3 always remain visible.
6. Save the file and close Excel.

33   Custom views

With custom views, you can save different views of a table and switch back and forth between these views. The following settings can be saved: Zoom factor, column widths, row heights, displayed and hidden columns and rows, filter settings or the window status (maximized or minimized). The current display is saved first. Rarely used columns are then hidden. This reduced display is saved as a second view.

Instruction

1. Open the sample file: ***Chapter 33 - Kitchen comparison - Start - B3***
2. Click on the ***View*** tab → ***Custom Views*** button to open the ***Custom Views*** dialog box.

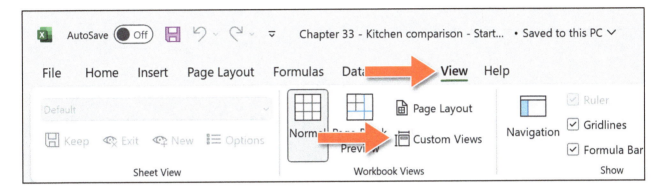

3. Click on the ***Add*** button in the ***Custom Views*** dialog box.

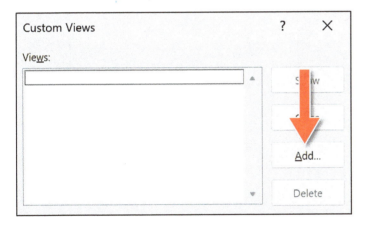

4. Enter the name ***Standard*** and click on the ***OK*** button to save the current view.

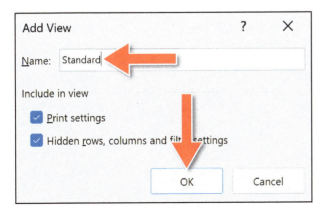

5. Place the mouse pointer on the header of column D and, holding down the left mouse button, drag the mouse to column K to select these columns.

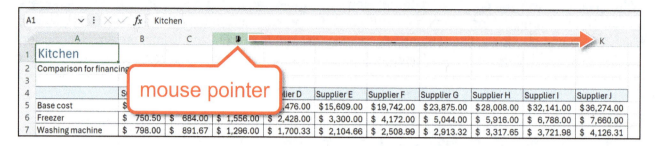

6. Right-click on one of the selected column headers to open the context menu. Click on the **Hide** list item in the context menu.

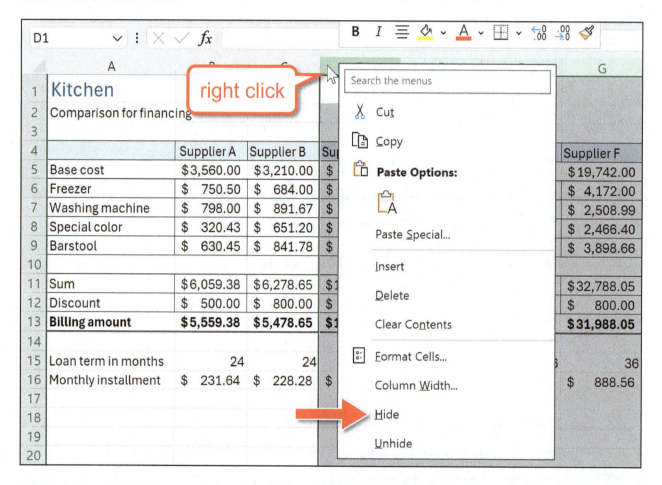

Advice: The data in these columns is rarely required. It should therefore be possible to show and hide them at the touch of a button.

7. In the **View** tab, click on the **Custom Views** button again.

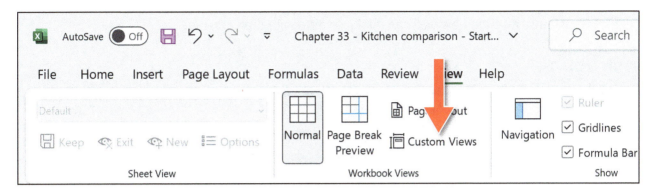

8. Click on the **Add** button again to add another custom view.

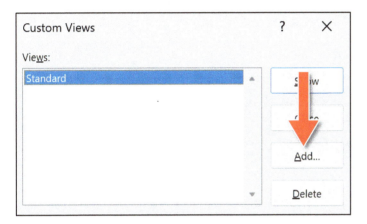

9. Enter the name **Reduced** for this custom view and confirm the entry with the **OK** button.

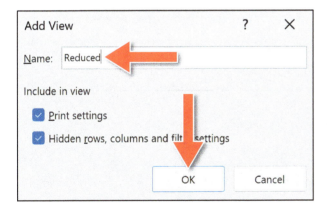

10. Click on the **Custom Views** button again.
11. Double-click on the **Standard** custom view to reactivate it.
    Result: Columns D to K are displayed again.
    Attention: Custom views are incompatible with smart tables. If you create a smart table in an Excel file, the custom views are automatically disabled.
12. Save the file and close Excel.

34   Evaluating data with pivot tables

These instructions describe how you can evaluate data with a pivot table.

Instruction

1. Open the sample file: ***Chapter 34 - Car list - Start - B3***
2. Place the cell pointer in any cell in the data range from A1 to G2033 to select this range.

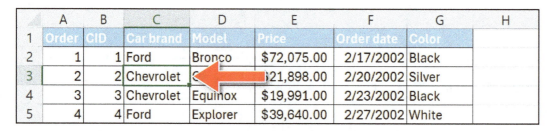

3. Click on the ***Insert*** tab.

4. Click on the ***Recommended PivotTables*** button to open the ***Recommended PivotTables*** dialog box.

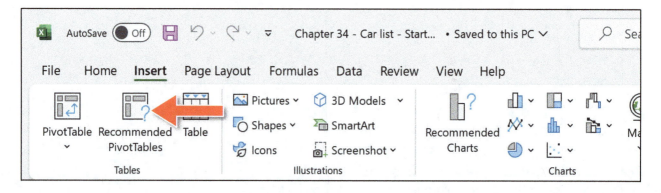

5. Look at the selected pivot table and click on the **OK** button to insert this table.

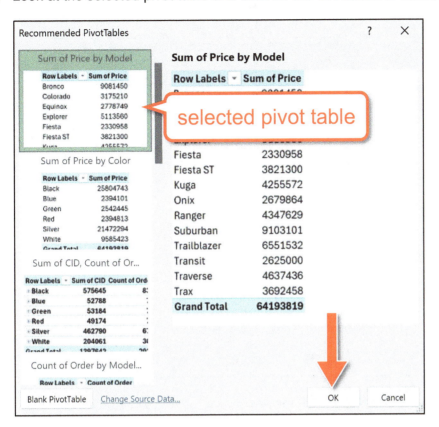

Advice: Also try out the other recommended pivot tables.

6. Look at the result.

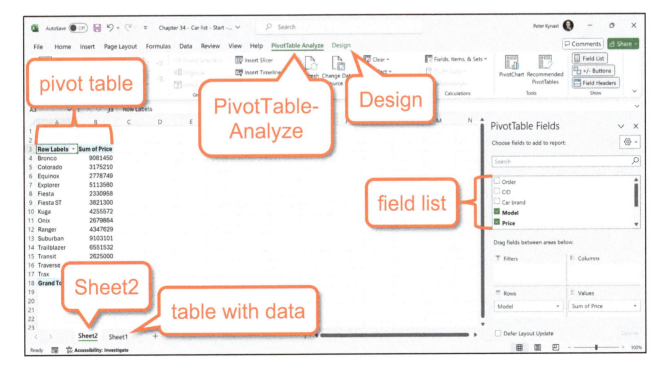

Result: The pivot table is inserted on a new sheet tab (Sheet2). The **PivotTable Analyze** and **Design** tabs are displayed when the cell pointer is in the pivot table. The **Model** and **Price** fields are currently selected.

7. Scroll down the field list using the scroll bar or the scroll wheel and activate the *Color* field. Look at the result.

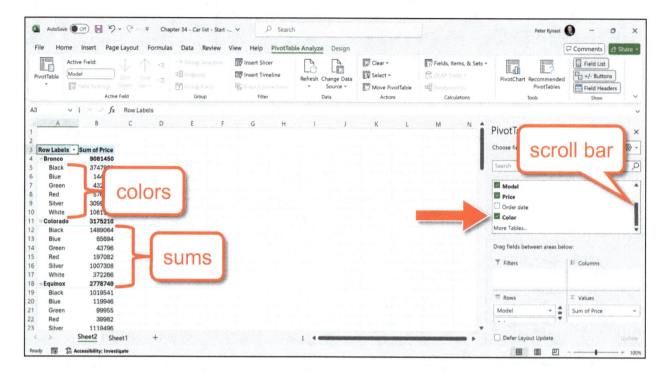

Result: The models are also divided into colors. Sums are calculated for the individual colors.

8. Save the file and close Excel.

Do you need help?

Do you have any questions about this book or Excel? Write us an email and we will be happy to help you personally! Please also look at our homepage on the internet. We have prepared some help topics for you there.

Email: info@ityco.com

Internet: www.ityco.com → Help

---

35   Quickly deleting multiple blank rows

These instructions describe how you can quickly select and delete several blank rows.

Instruction

1. Open the sample file: ***Chapter 35 - Departments - Start - B3***
2. In the ***Home*** tab, click on the ***Find & Select*** button and then on the ***Go To Special*** list item to open the ***Go To Special*** dialog box.

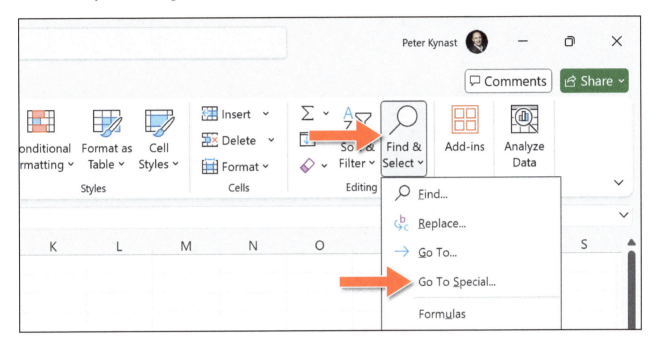

3. Activate ***Blanks*** and click on the ***OK*** button.

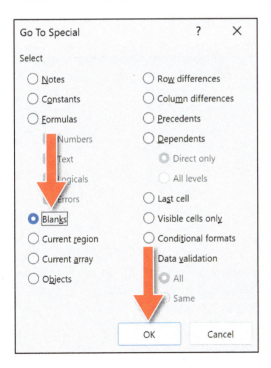

     Result: The empty rows in the data area are selected.

4. Click on the *Delete* button to delete the selected rows.

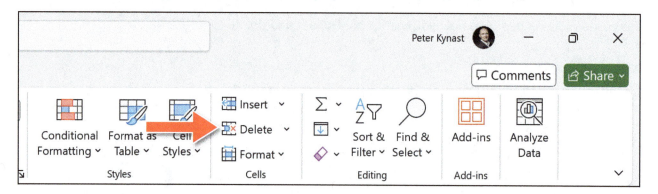

5. Look at the result.

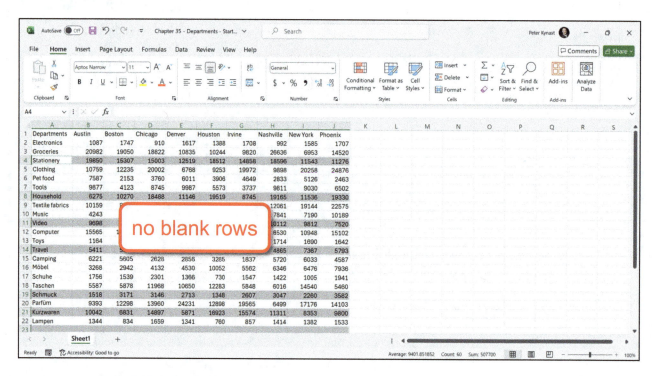

Result: All empty cells are deleted.

6. Save the file and close Excel.

Repetitions

Repetitions are crucial when learning! We therefore recommend working through this book at least **twice** to consolidate your new knowledge.

36 Line break in a cell

These instructions describe how you can insert a line break (word wrap) in a cell.

Instruction

1. Open the sample file: *Chapter 36 - Data usage - Start - B3*
2. Enter the word *Sum* in B18. However, do <u>not</u> press the *enter key* ↵ yet.

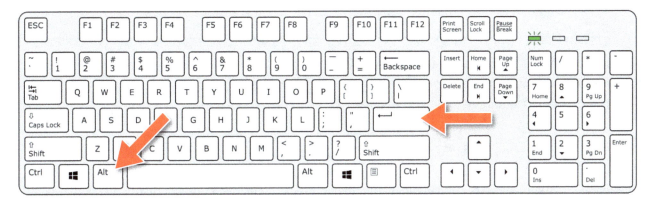

3. Press the key combination ⏎ Alt + *enter key* ↵ to insert a line break.

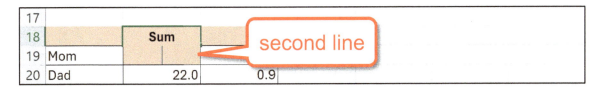

Advice: The following applies to button combinations consisting of 2 buttons: Press and hold the first button and then briefly press the second button. Then release the first button again.

4. Look at the result.

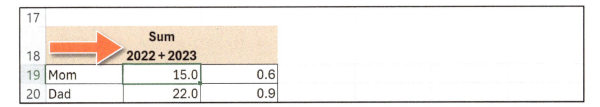

Result: A second line is created in cell B18. The cursor flashes in this line.

5. Enter *2022 + 2023* and press the *enter key* ↵ to confirm the entry. Look at the result.

Result: Edit mode is exited. The height of the row is doubled. The text *2022 + 2023* is displayed in the second line of the cell. However, it still belongs to the same cell.

6. Save the file and close Excel.

37   Swapping rows and columns in tables

Long tables are often clearer and easier to use than wide tables. One reason for this is that long tables are easier to scroll with the mouse. In addition, there are techniques that can only be applied to vertical (long) tables, e.g. filters. This guide describes how to swap rows and columns in tables. In this way, you can convert a wide table into a long table.

Instruction

1. Open the sample file: **Chapter 37 - Employees - Start - B3**
2. Look at the table. The data is arranged horizontally (sideways).

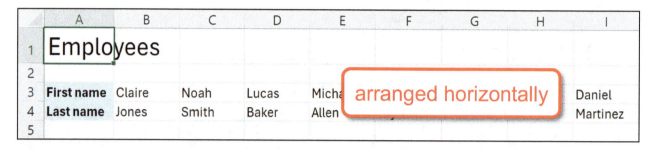

3. Click on any cell in the range from A3 to Z4.
4. Press the key combination **control key** `Ctrl` + `A` to select the whole data range.
5. Click on the **Copy** button to copy this data.

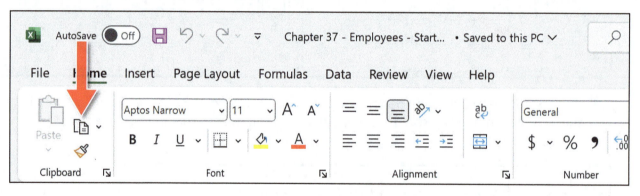

6. Select cell A6. The data should be inserted at this position.
7. Click on the small arrow under the **Paste** button to open the list box for this button.

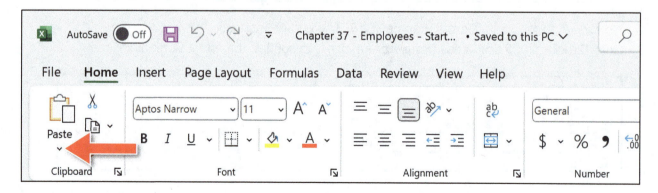

© 2024 - www.ityco.com

8. Click on the *Transpose* button to paste the data as columns.

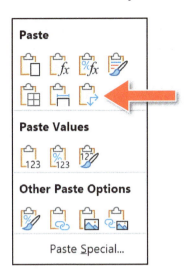

9. Undo the selection and look at the result.

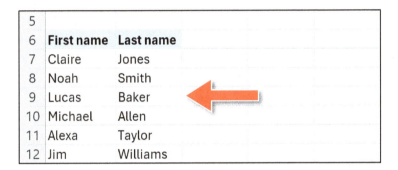

Result: The table is inserted in the area A6 to B31. First names and surnames are now displayed in columns.

10. Select the row headers of row 2 to 4 and click on the *Delete* button ⊞ to delete the old data.

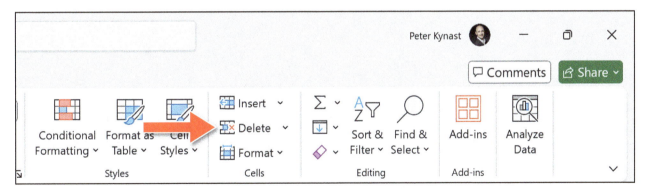

11. Save the file and close Excel.

38   Find and replace

These instructions describe how you can delete brackets from a list of telephone numbers using the Find and replace function. This example can be applied to many other situations.

Instruction

1. Open the sample file: *Chapter 38 - Phone numbers - Start - B3*
2. Click on the *Find & Select* button to open this list box.

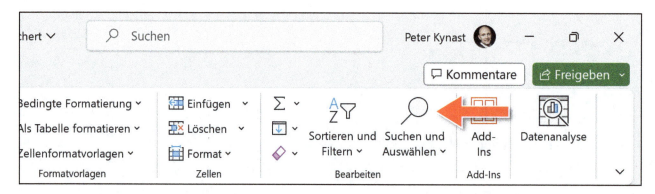

3. Click on the *Replace* list item to open the *Replace* dialog box.

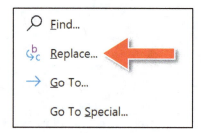

4. Enter a single space into the *Find what* field.

5. Click on the **Replace all** button and look at the result.

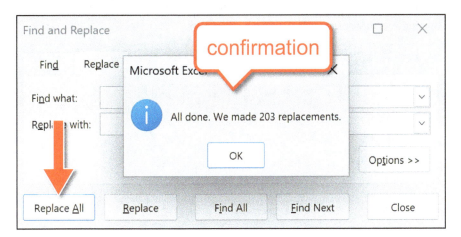

Result: Since the **Replace with** field is empty, every blank space in the table is deleted.

6. Confirm the message with the **OK** button.
7. Repeat the process with a closing bracket **)** in the **Find what** field and a closing bracket **)** followed by a blank space in the **Replace with** field. Look at the result. You can insert the closing bracket by pressing the key combination **shift key** ⇧ + 0 .

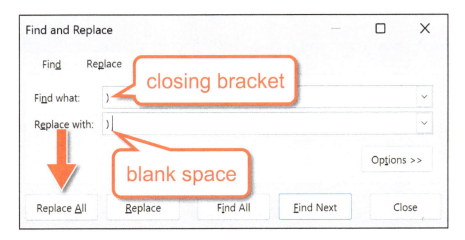

Result: A blank space is inserted after every closing bracket.

8. Close both dialog boxes and look at the table.

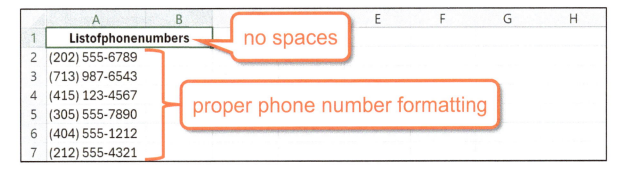

Result: The phone numbers are displayed with a blank space after the closing brackets and no excess spaces around the hyphen. However, the heading also lost the spaces between each word.

9. Insert a space after **List**, **of** and **phone** in A1 to fix the heading.
10. Save the file and close Excel.

39   Calculating with dates 1

These instructions describe the basics required for calculating with dates.

Instruction

1. Open Excel with an empty workbook and enter the following data.

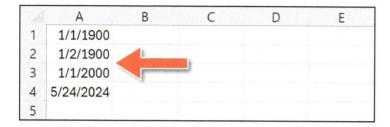

2. Select the range from A1 to A4 and look at the **Number Format** list box.

Result: The list box displays the **Date** number format.
Advice: Every date is a number in Excel! Excel's time calculation begins with the date 1/1/1900. This is day 1 for Excel. This date corresponds to the value 1. 1/2/1900 corresponds to the value 2. 1/3/1900 corresponds to the value 3 and so on. If you enter a date in a cell, Excel automatically assigns the **Date** format to this cell. A date is therefore a number with the date format. An amount of money, e.g. $ 20.00, is a number with the number format **Dollar**.

3. Open the **Number Format** list box and click on the **General** list item to remove the **Date** format. Look at the result.

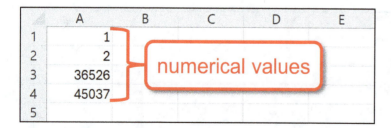

Result: The date format is removed. Excel displays the numerical values of these cells.
Advice: There are 100 years between the dates 1/1/1900 and 1/0/2000. A year has 365 days. There were 26 leap years (years with 366 days) in this period. Therefore the number 36526 is displayed in A3. 100 x 365 + 26 = 36526. Between 1/1/1900 and 1/1/2000 are 36526 days. There are 45436 days between 1/1/1900 and 5/24/2024

4. Close Excel without saving.

40   Calculating with dates 2

These instructions describe how you can calculate with dates.

Instruction

1. Open the sample file: ***Chapter 40 - Delivery date - Start - B3***

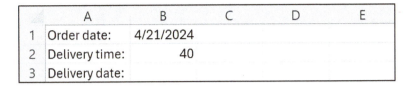

2. Enter the formula ***=B1+B2*** in B3 to calculate the delivery date.

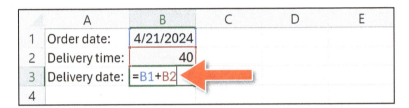

   Advice: In Excel every date is a number! This means you can calculate with dates. In this example, 40 days are added to the date 4/21/2024 to calculate the delivery date.

3. Look at the result.

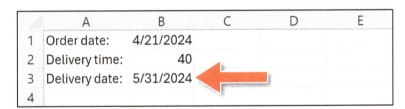

   Result: Excel recognizes the date format in B1. Therefore, the date format is also assigned to B3. The calculated date is 5/31/2024.

4. Enter the formula ***=B3-B1*** in B4 to carry out the cross-check.

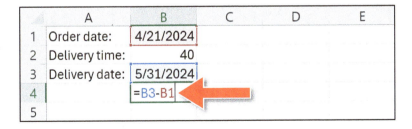

   Advice: The date 4/21/2024 is closer to 1/1/1900 than 5/31/2024. Therefore, the date 4/21/2024 is the smaller number and 5/31/24 is the larger number. You therefore calculate ***=B3-B1*** and not ***=B1-B3*** (larger number minus the smaller number).

5. Press the ***enter key*** ⏎ and look at the result.
   Result: B4 displays the result 40.
6. Save the file and close Excel.

41   Filling multiple cells at once

These instructions describe how you can insert a value into multiple cells at the same time.

Instruction

1. Open the sample file: ***Chapter 41 - Work hours - Start - B3***
2. Select the cell range C4 to C16.
3. Enter the time ***8:00 AM***. However, do <u>not</u> complete the entry yet.

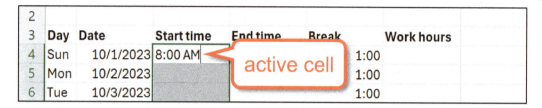

Advice: The entry is automatically made in C4, as C4 is the active cell. You can always recognize the active cell by the transparent selection. The fill color of the cell is visible.

4. Press the key combination ***control key*** Ctrl + ***enter key*** ↵ to fill all selected cells with this time.

5. Look at the result.

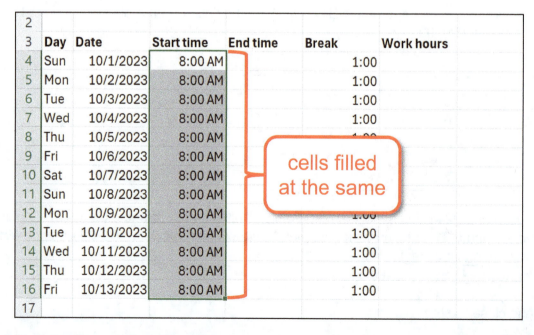

6. Save the file and close Excel.

---

42   Creating custom number formats

Excel offers a range of preset number formats, e.g. dollar, percentage or fraction, but the choice is limited. By default, Excel does not have a number format for miles or pounds. If you want to use these or other number formats, you must create a custom number format.

Instruction

1. Open the sample file: ***Chapter 42 - Running progress - Start - B3***
2. Select the cell range B5 to C28.
3. Click on the arrow 🔽 in the **Number** area to open the **Format Cells** dialog box.

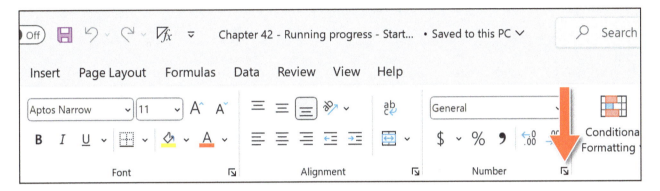

4. Click on the **Custom** category on the left-hand side.
5. Click into the **Type** input field to activate edit mode.
6. Delete the word ***General*** and enter ***0.0 "mi"***. Pay attention to the quotation marks!

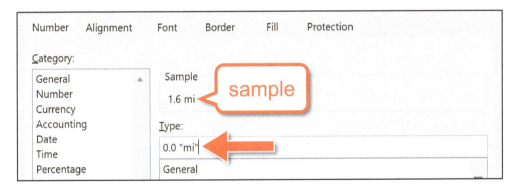

7. Click on the **OK** button to assign the new format to the selected area.
8. Undo the selection and look at the result.

4		Best run	Worst run
5	Week 13	1.6 mi	0.9 mi
6	Week 14	1.8 mi	1.3 mi
7	Week 15	2.5 mi	1.9 mi
8	Week 16	1.4 mi	0.9 mi

Result: All numbers are given the unit ***mi*** (miles). You can calculate with these cells! If you had typed the unit ***mi*** into the cells, Excel does not recognize the entry as a number and cannot use these cells for calculations.

9. Save the file and close Excel.

43   Conditional formatting

These instructions describe how you can automatically assign formats to emphasize higher values.

Instruction

1. Open the sample file: ***Chapter 43 - Company cars - Start - B3***
2. Select the area B4 to N22.

   Advice: If you place the cell pointer in B4 and press the key combination ***control key*** `Ctrl` + ***shift key*** `⇧` + `End`, the cell range from B4 to the end of the table will be selected.
3. Click on the ***Conditional Formatting*** button in the ***Home*** tab.

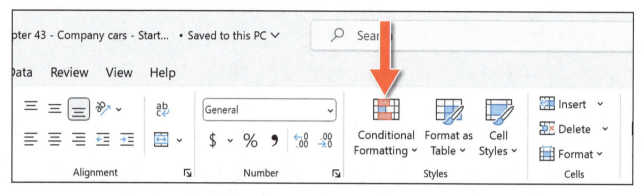

4. Click on the ***Red - White Color Scale*** conditional formatting in the ***Color scales*** area.

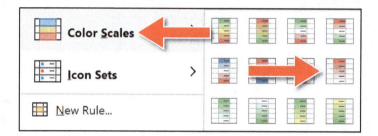

5. Undo the selection and look at the result.

3 Car / year	2011	2012	2013	2014	2015	2016	2017	2018	2019	2020	2021	2022	2023
4 SJD 012	594	827	2378	242	2740	1004	35	1045	2544	629	1968	657	1158
5 SJD 013	2140	2886	2254	1329	643	709	920	386	1774	1570	2869	1917	1377
6 SJD 014	1577	1558	209	1690	76	774	0	746	709	1246	192	97	940
7 SJD 015	201	1744	2343	2937	1054	1055	2828	2613	2243	485	71	1374	1943
8 SJD 016	2539	2557	149	1204	0	1845	2375	1031	1751	30	2667	1828	1548
9 SJD 017	1688	2538	1482	1318	1279	30	881	1049	623	1252	1053	1495	6203
10 SJD 018	542	1170	524	439	408	1860	1062	2963	919	2363	1908	2863	2827
11 SJD 019	2182	1523	2520	385	1374	318	66	2384	429	2856	1375	2939	1766
12 SJD 020	2265	1837	1352	1659	291	2495	1492	80	2335	1511	6347	2457	495
13 SJD 021	483	2878	1528	2581	736	221	268	2674	591	2475	449	1360	1856
14 SJD 022					939	889	1606	2186	2819	1823	2160	347	1778
15 SJD 023					838	2348	1957	6250	1383	1131	822	2517	2669
16 SJD 024					154	93	2201	1039	671	328	1756	994	1753
17 SJD 025					209	735	1710	426	1778	248	863	1668	1638
18 SJD 026					524	2085	71	1968	450	758	201	1377	2035
19 SJD 027	2672		377	2035	754	2759	1773	108	2434	1768	1589	1885	2436
20 SJD 028	2610	1909	532	1748	1197	2567	1988	469	748	651	1949	2651	1403
21 SJD 029	410	6878	2902	2379	679	209	363	2968	1006	2436	521	2891	1604
22 SJD 030	1139	909	1359	1160	113	1372	2008	2445	1353	2605	2892	2163	2549

highest value

Result: The ***Red - White Color Scale*** formats low values with a white background. The higher the value, the stronger the red tone.

6. Save the file and close Excel.

44   Adding buttons to the quick access toolbar

These instructions describe how you can add any buttons to the quick access toolbar. The quick access toolbar is located at the top left of the program window and can be assigned frequently used buttons by the user.

Instruction

1. Open Excel with any workbook.
2. In the **Formulas** tab, <u>right-click</u> on the **Show Formulas** button to display the context menu.

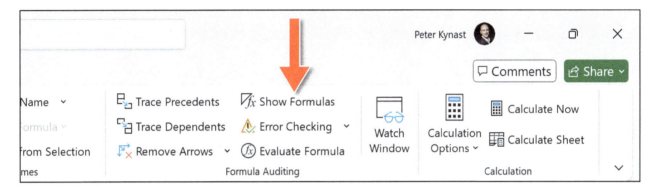

3. Click on the **Add to Quick Access Toolbar** list item in the context menu.

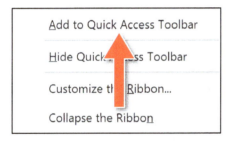

4. Look at the result.

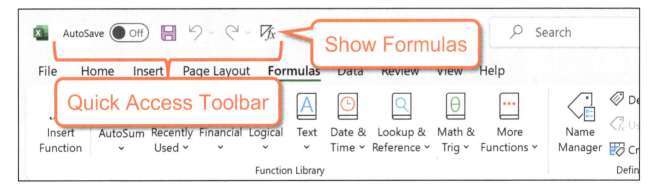

Result: The **Show Formulas** button is displayed in the **Quick Access Toolbar**.
Advice: You can add almost any button to the quick access toolbar in this way. To remove a button from the quick access toolbar, right-click the button → **Remove from Quick Access Toolbar**.

5. Close Excel without saving.
Advice: Button configurations in the quick access toolbar are saved automatically and are not tied to the current workbook.

45   Navigate to cells via the name field

Imagine a colleague draws your attention to an error in a table. The error is in cell Z335. The table is very large and you want to get to the cell you are looking for quickly. These instructions describe how you can use the name field to do this.

Instruction

1. Open the sample file: *Chapter 45 - Sales - Start - B3*
2. Click in the name field.

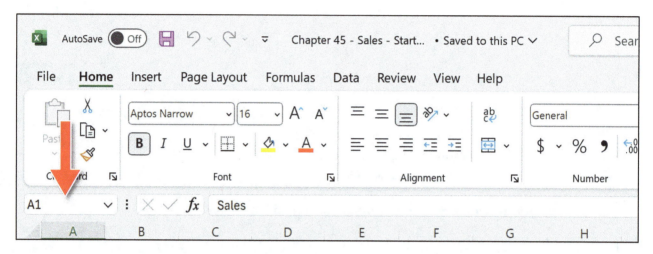

3. Enter the cell name *Z335* in the name field.

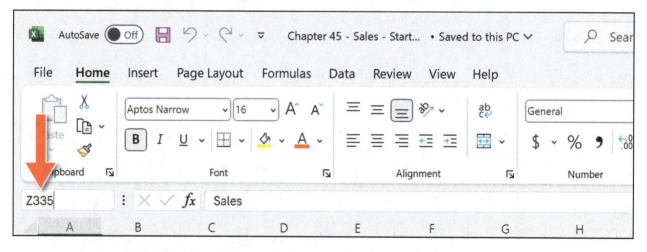

4. Press the *enter key* ⏎ and look at the result.

14807	14122	10941	5348	9862	6275
11463	11262	4984	5969	8278	8360
10575	6765		1034500	13985	8676
2364	2669	3723	5035	2510	3760

Result: The cell Z335 is selected.

5. Enter the value *10345* in this cell and confirm the entry.
6. Save the file and close Excel.

46   Using the arrow keys when correcting cell values

If you press an arrow key when making a <u>new entry</u>, this will end edit mode. These instructions describe how you can still use the arrow keys for correction purposes.

Instruction

1. Open Excel with an empty workbook.
   Enter the word **Invoce** in A1. <u>Deliberately</u> misspell the word. However, do not press the **enter key** ↵ yet.

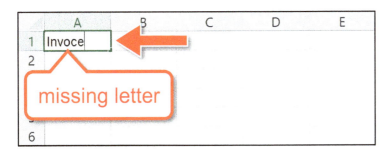

Attention: If you were to press the **left arrow key** ← now, the entry would be confirmed.

2. Press the **function key** F2.

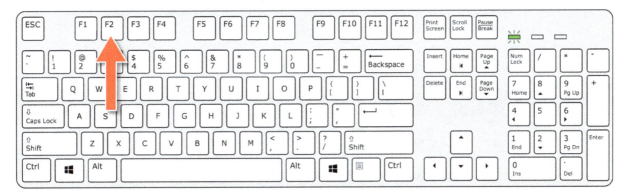

Result: By pressing the **function key** F2, you can move the cursor within the text by using the arrow keys.

3. Navigate to the position of the mistake by pressing the **left arrow key** ← twice.

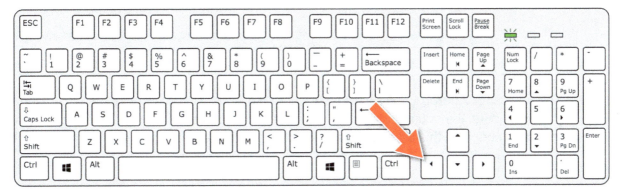

4. Enter the missing letter **i** and confirm the entry with the **enter key** ↵.
5. Close Excel without saving.

47   Reading results on the status bar 1

These instructions describe how you can use the status bar for simple evaluations.

Instruction

1. Open the sample file: *Chapter 47 - Work hours - B3*
2. Select the area F4 to F29.

18	Thu	1/18/2024	8:00 AM	4:00 PM	1:00	7:00
19	Fri	1/19/2024	8:00 AM	4:00 PM	1:00	7:00
20	Sat	1/20/2024	8:00 AM	3:30 PM	1:00	6:30
21	Mon	1/22/2024	8:00 AM	4:06 PM	1:00	7:06
22	Tue	1/23/2024	8:00 AM	4:00 PM	1:00	7:00
23	Wed	1/24/2024	8:00 AM	5:15 PM	1:00	8:15
24	Thu	1/25/2024	8:00 AM	4:00 PM	1:00	7:00
25	Fri	1/26/2024	8:00 AM	4:00 PM	1:00	7:00
26	Sat	1/27/2024	8:00 AM	6:15 PM	1:00	9:15
27	Mon	1/29/2024	8:00 AM	4:00 PM	1:00	7:00
28	Tue	1/30/2024	8:00 AM	4:00 PM	1:00	7:00
29	Wed	1/31/2024	8:00 AM	8:00 PM	1:00	11:00

26R x 1C

Sheet1 +

Ready   Accessibility: Good to go

3. Look at the status bar in the bottom right of the Excel program window.

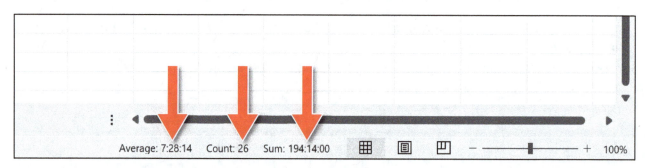

Average: 7:28:14   Count: 26   Sum: 194:14:00   100%

Result: The results for *Average*, *Count* and *Sum* are displayed. The average value shows the average number of hours, the count shows the number of cell contents and the total shows the total number of working hours in this area. Selecting the cells is sufficient for these evaluations. You do not need to enter any formulas.

4. Close Excel without saving.

48 Reading results on the status bar 2

The average value, count and sum evaluations are displayed on the status bar by default. These instructions describe how you can display further evaluations on this bar.

Instruction

1. Open the sample file: ***Chapter 48 - Recruitment - B3***
2. <u>Right-click</u> on the status bar to open the context menu.

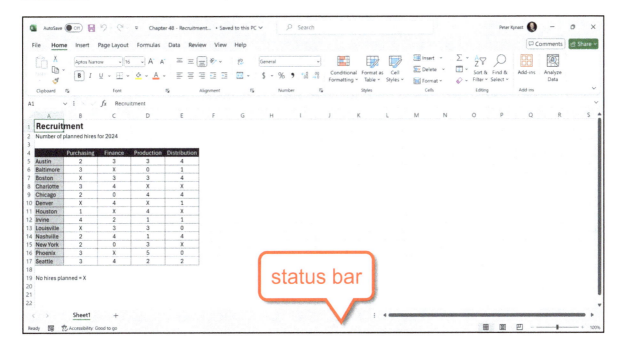

Advice: The status bar is located at the bottom of the excel program window.

3. Click on the ***Numerical Count*** list item to add this calculation to the status bar.

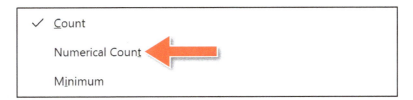

4. Select the area B5 to E17 and look at the status bar. You want to know how often an ***X*** has been entered (departments that have no planned hiring).

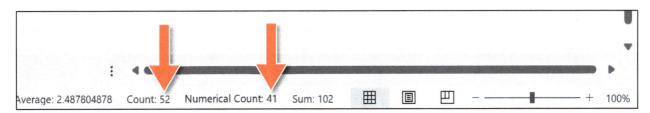

Result: The evaluation on the status bar shows that the selected area contains a total of 52 texts and numbers. Of this data, 41 are numerical data (numbers). This area therefore contains the X 11 times (52 total values minus 41 numerical values = 11)

5. Close Excel without saving.

49   Adding work hours

By default, Excel interprets times as 24 hour clock times. A problem arises when adding these times. As soon as the total exceeds the value 23:59:59, the displayed time starts again at 00:00:00. This guide describes how you can add up hours if the total is greater than or equal to 24 hours.

Instruction

1. Open the sample file: ***Chapter 49 - Time tracking - Start - B3***
2. Click on cell F30 and look at the result.

26	Mon	2/27/2023	8:00 AM	8:00 PM	1:00	11:00	
27	Tue	2/28/2023	8:15 AM	4:45 PM	1:00	7:30	
28	Total					**20:17**	
29							
30							

Advice: The displayed result is incorrect.

3. Look at the formula in the formula bar.

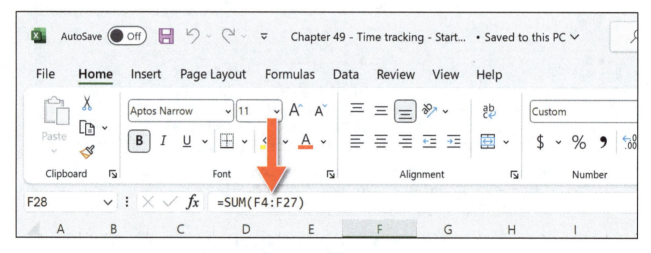

Advice: This formula is correct! The incorrect result is due to the wrong time format.

4. Click on the small arrow ⤢ in the **Number** area to open the **Format Cells** dialog box.

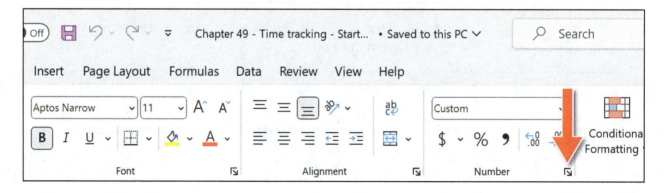

5. Click on the *Time* category and then on the list item **37:30:55**.

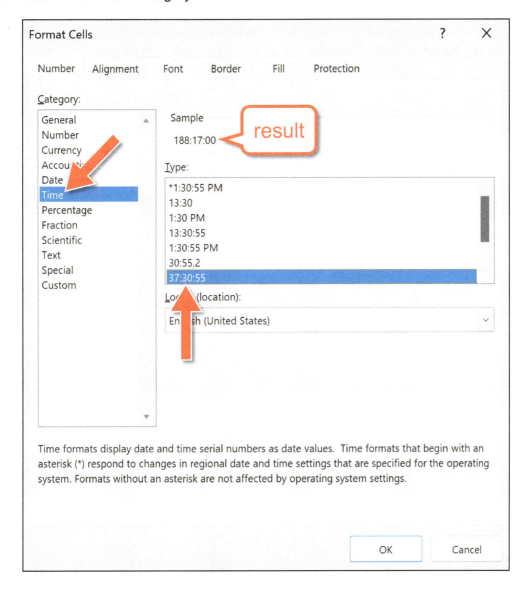

Result: The result in the *Sample* area already shows the correct result. It results from the selected cell (F30) and the selected format **37:30:55**.
Advice: The **37:30:55** format is used for times that go beyond the 24-hour rhythm.
6. Click on the *OK* button to accept the new format.
7. Look at the result.

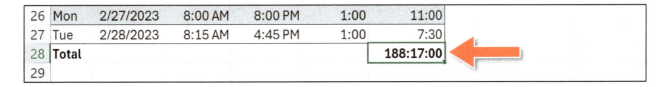

26	Mon	2/27/2023	8:00 AM	8:00 PM	1:00	11:00
27	Tue	2/28/2023	8:15 AM	4:45 PM	1:00	7:30
28	**Total**					**188:17:00**
29						

Result: The total number of hours is displayed correctly.
Advice: If you want to delete the two digits for the seconds, open the *Format Cells* window again. In the *Numbers* tab, click on the *Custom* category. In the *Type* field, change the format **[h]:mm:ss;@** to **[h]:mm;@** or **[h]:mm**.
8. Save the file and close Excel.

50   Selecting 1 - Extending selections

These instructions describe how you can select a large area without dragging with the mouse. This method can be helpful for large and confusing tables.

Instruction

1. Open the sample file: ***Chapter 50 - Mileage - Start - B3***
2. Place the cell pointer on cell A3.
3. Press the ***function key*** F8 to activate the so-called ***Extend Mode***.

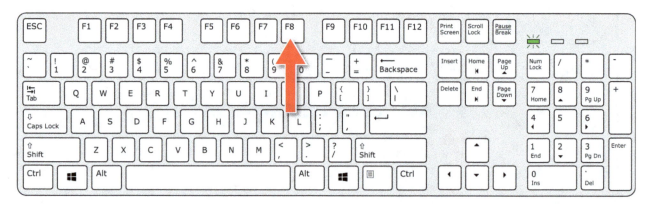

4. Look at the status bar at the bottom of the Excel window. It displays the text ***Extend Selection***.

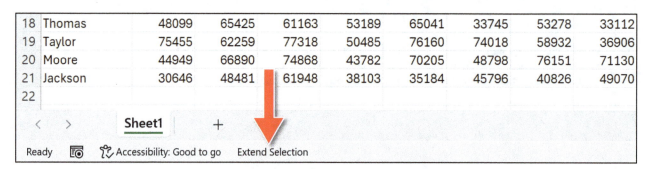

5. Scroll to the end of the table and click on the last cell with content (cell X362) to create a selection from A3 to X362.

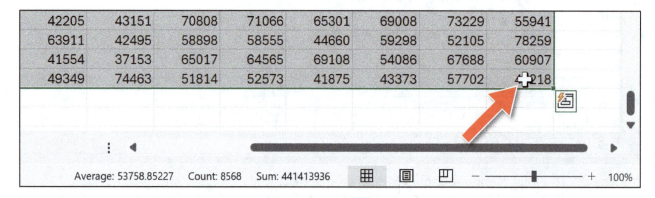

6. Press the ***function key*** F8 again to exit the extend mode.
7. Assign the ***All Borders*** format to the cell range.
8. Save the file and close Excel.

51   Selecting 2 - Reducing a selection

Up to and including Excel 2016, it was not possible to resize an existing selection with the mouse. All versions from Excel 2019 onwards now support this technique.

Instruction

1. Open the sample file: ***Chapter 51 - Students - Start - B3***
2. Select the cell range A3 to E7.

	Enrollment 2020	Enrollment 2021	Enrollment 2022	Enrollment 2023
Summerville Academy	86	143	116	82
Apple Valley High	152	159	109	113
Dallas Tech	102	149	118	157
Sums	340	451	343	352

3. Press and hold the ***control key*** Ctrl .
4. Click on the cell A3 to remove this cell from the selection. Look at the result.

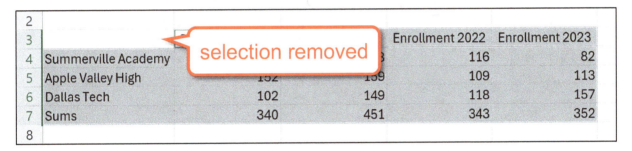

5. Continue to hold down the ***control key*** Ctrl . Click on the cell A7 and drag the mouse to cell E7, to remove these cells from the selection as well.

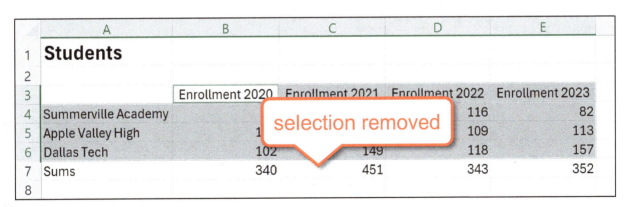

Attention: If you want to reduce the size of an existing selection, you must set the starting point in-side the selection. If you start outside the existing selection, e.g. A8, you would add cells to the selection instead.

6. Assign the ***All Borders*** format to the cell range area and undo the selection.
7. Save the file and close Excel.

52 Adding whole columns or rows

These instructions describe how you can calculate with whole columns or rows.

Instruction

1. Open the sample file: ***Chapter 52 - Sum - Start - B3***
2. Enter the formula **=SUM(A:A)** in cell B1 to calculate the sum of the entire column A.

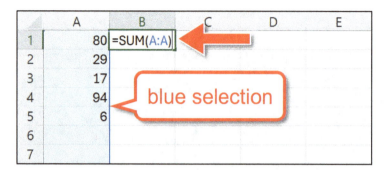

blue selection

Advice: With the range specification A:A, you select the entire column A. This involves 1048576 cells. The blue marking highlights the selected range.

Attention: The cell with the formula must not be in column A itself! This would create a so-called ***circular reference***. Circular reference means: The formula includes its own cell. It is in a loop. An error message appears in this case. The formula must be corrected.

3. Look at the result.

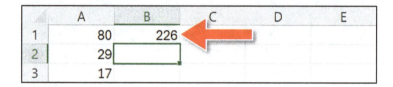

4. Enter another number in column A and look at the result.

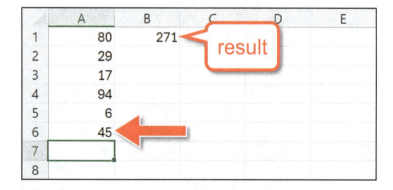

result

Result: The result includes the new value.

Example: Look at the following examples.

=SUM(A:B)	Adds all values in the two columns A and B.
=SUM(1:1)	Adds all values in row 1.
=COUNT(A:F)	Counts all numbers in columns A to F.
=AVERAGE(1:3)	Calculates the average of all values in rows 1, 2 and 3.

5. Save the file and close Excel.

53 Automatic completion of function names with the tab key

These instructions describe how you can quickly insert function names without having to write them out.

Instruction

1. Open the sample file: *Chapter 53 - Average - Start - B3*
2. Enter the partial formula *=av* in cell A4.

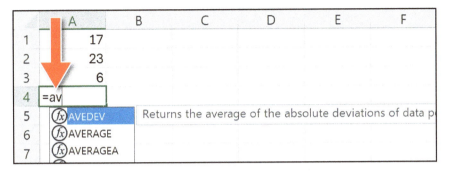

3. Press the *down arrow key* ↓ to select the *AVERAGE* function in the list.

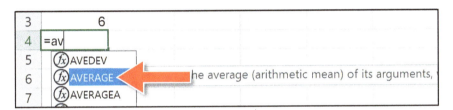

4. Press the *tab key* ⇆ to accept the function from the list.

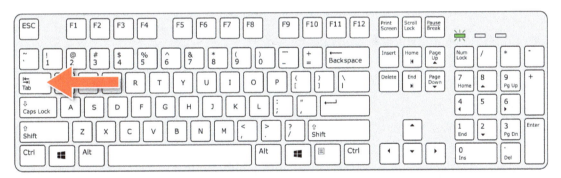

Result: The function is written out in full. The opening bracket is also inserted.

Attention: The *enter key* ↵ cannot be used for this process. However, you can also select the desired function by double-clicking on it.

5. Look at the result.

6. Complete the function as follows and complete the entry: *=AVERAGE(A1:A3)*
7. Save the file and close Excel.

54 Navigating with many tables 1

These instructions describe how you can quickly switch to another sheet tab in workbooks with many sheets.

Instruction

1. Open the sample file: **Chapter 54 - Coffee - B3**
2. <u>Right-click</u> on the navigation arrows for the table tabs in the bottom left of the excel window.

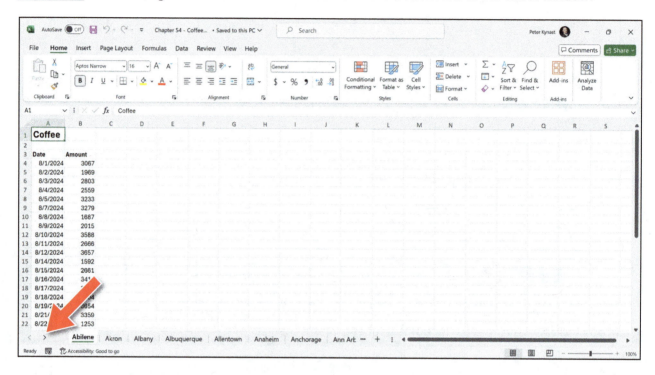

Result: A list with all tables in the Excel file is displayed.

3. Scroll down and <u>double-click</u> on **Omaha** to activate this table.

4. Close Excel without saving.

55   Navigating with many tables 2

These instructions describe how you can quickly access the last or first few tables.

Instruction

1. Open the sample file: ***Chapter 55 - Coffee - B3***
2. Press and hold the ***control key*** Ctrl .

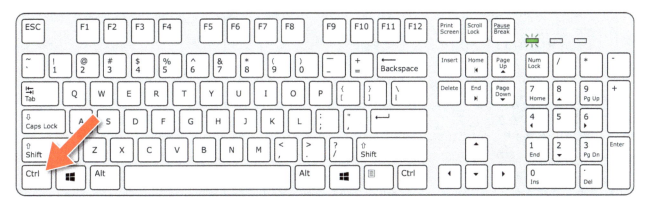

3. Left-click on the right-hand navigation arrow for the sheet tabs to see the last tables of the Excel file.

4. Release the ***control key*** Ctrl and look at the result.

Result: The last table tabs of this Excel worksheet are displayed.

Advice: If you click on the left arrow while pressing the ***control key*** Ctrl , the first tables of the worksheet are displayed.

5. Close Excel without saving.

56   Copying formats multiple times

These instructions describe how you can copy formats multiple times to other cells.

Instruction

1. Open the sample file: **Chapter 56 - Quarterly figures - Start - B3**
2. Select the cell range A3 to B8.

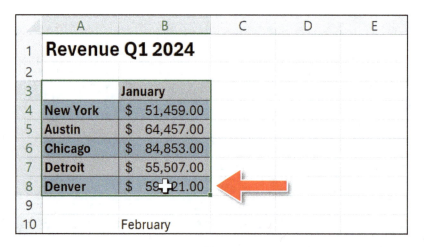

Advice: The formats of this table should be copied to the February and March tables.

3. Underline-<u>Double-click</u> on the **Format Painter** button.

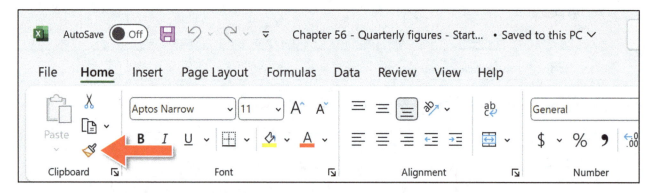

Result: The **Format Painter** button is active and is therefore highlighted in gray. The selected area is highlighted by an animated frame.
Advice: If you only click on the **Format Painter** button once, the format can only be copied <u>once</u>. The function is then automatically deactivated again. You can copy the format <u>multiple times</u> by double-clicking on the **Format Painter** button.

4. Click on cell A10 to copy the format to the month of February.

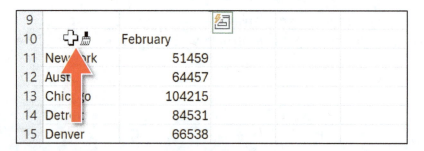

5. Look at the result.

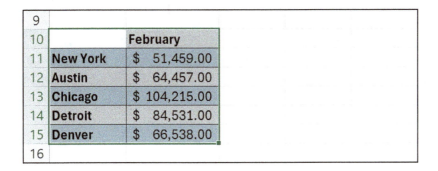

Result: The formats are copied. The entire table area is selected.

Advice: During this process, the tables you are formatting must be of the same size!

6. Click on cell A17 to copy the format to the month of **March**.

7. Click on the **Format Painter** button again to exit the mode.

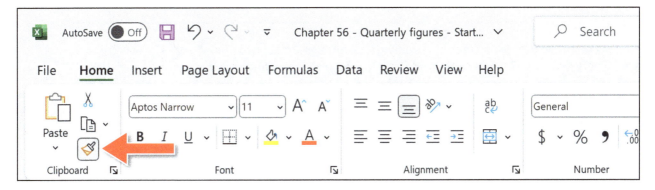

Or: Press the **escape key** Esc to exit the **Format painter** mode.

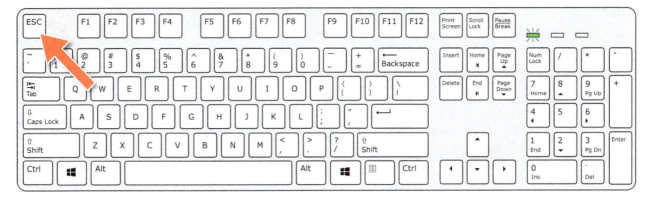

8. Save the file and close Excel.

57   Adjusting column widths to the content

These instructions describe how you can adjust column widths to the content. Column widths are specified in units of characters. A Width of 3 provides space for 3 characters of average width. However, the characters are not all the same width. Example: A **W** is wider than an *i*. We therefore recommend that you allow for a buffer. If you want to enter up to 3 characters in the cells, set the width to 4.

Instruction

1. Open the sample file: ***Chapter 57 - Multiplication table - Start - B3***
2. Point to the column header of column A with the mouse A.

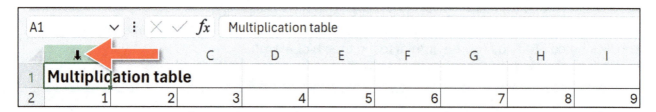

Result: The mouse pointer is displayed as a black arrow pointing down ↓.

3. Hold down the mouse button and drag to column J to select these columns.

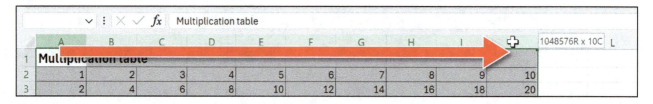

4. Click on the **Format** button and then on the **Column Width** list item.

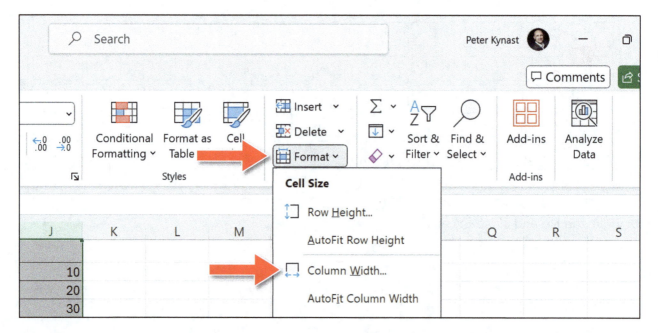

5. Enter the value **4** and confirm the entry by clicking on the **OK** button. Look at the result.
   Result: Column width 4 is set for all selected columns.
6. Save the file and close Excel.

58   Adjusting the width of multiple columns at once

These instructions describe how you can adjust the width of several columns to their content at the same time.

Instruction

1. Open the sample file: ***Chapter 58 - Temperatures - Start - B3***
2. Point to the column header of column A with the mouse.

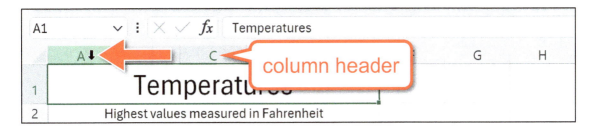

Result: The mouse pointer is displayed as a black arrow pointing down ↓.

3. Press and hold the mouse button and drag the mouse to column E to select the columns.

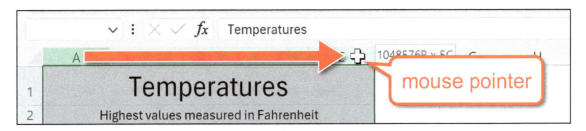

Result: The mouse pointer is displayed as a white cross ✛ while dragging.

4. Place the mouse pointer on a dividing line between the selected column headers.

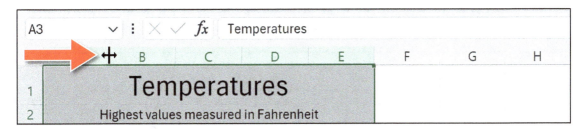

Result: The mouse pointer is displayed as a black double arrow ↔.

5. Double-click at this position to adjust the column width.
6. Undo the selection and look at the result.

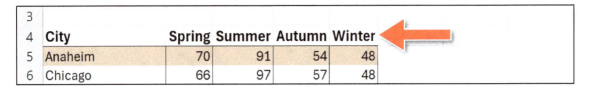

Result: The column widths are automatically adjusted to the longest content in the column. Connected headings, such as the heading ***Temperatures***, are ignored.

7. Save the file and close Excel.

59   Creating drop-down lists for cells

These instructions describe how you can create drop-down lists in cells. You can use drop-down lists to speed up and restrict the entries in a cell.

Instruction

1. Open the sample file: ***Chapter 59 - Concert tickets - Start - B3***
2. Select the cell range B4 to B12.

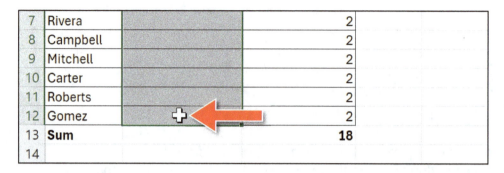

Advice: Only artists listed under the table in the area B17 to B22 should be able to be entered in this area.

3. Click on the ***Data*** tab.

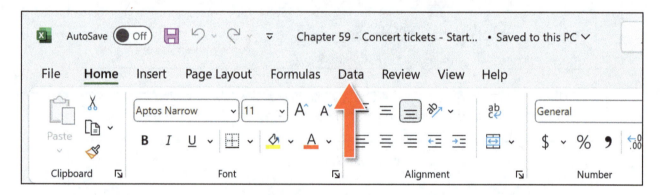

4. Click on the ***Data Validation*** button ⊡ to open the ***Data Validation*** dialog box.

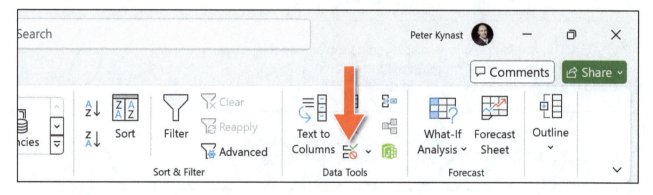

Advice: Data validation can be used to restrict the entries to cells.

5. Open the **Allow** list box and select the **List** list item.

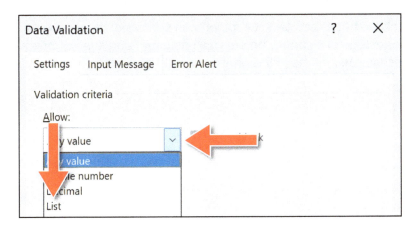

Result: This selection causes the **Source** field to be displayed.

6. Place the cursor inside the **Source** field.

7. Click on the table and select A17 to A22. Look at the result.

Result: The range is inserted in the notation **=$A$17:$A$22**.

8. Click on the **OK** button.
9. Click on the small arrow next to cell B4 to open the drop-down list for this cell.

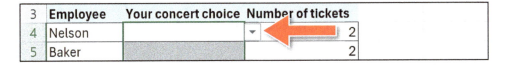

10. Click on an artist in the list to enter them in B4.

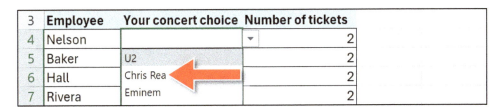

Advice: If you try to type other content into cells B4 to B12, you will receive an error message. Only the names in the list are accepted. To allow other entries, select the range B4 to B12 again and open the **Data Validation** dialog box → **Error Alert** tab. Change the type from **Stop** to **Information**.

11. Save the file and close Excel.

---

60   Centering texts over cells

The **Merge & Center** format is very practical, but it can lead to problems in some situations, e.g. when selecting or sorting cells. Areas with connected cells cannot be selected as usual and it is not possible to sort areas with connected cells. These instructions describe another way to center texts over cells.

Instruction

1. Open the sample file: **Chapter 60 - Tickets - Start - B3**
   Advice: You want to format all texts in column A in bold.
2. Click on cell A3 and look at the depiction.

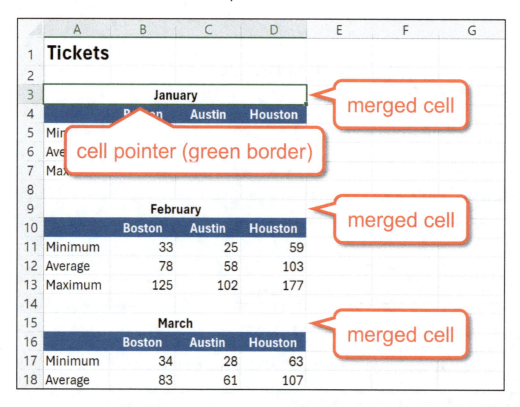

Result: The range A3 to D3 is a connected cell. It has been assigned the join and center format. You can recognize the connection by the green frame. It extends from A3 to D3. A9 and A15 are also merged.

3. Also click on A9 and A15 and check the formats.
   Result: The **Merge & Center** format was also assigned to these cells.
4. Select the cell range A5 to A8.

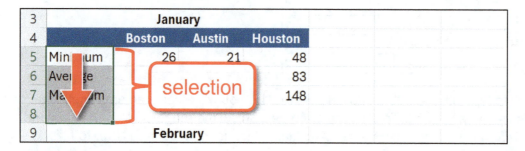

Result: This selection does not cause any problems. Only the cells from A5 to A8 are selected.

5. Select the cell range A5 to A9 and look at the result.

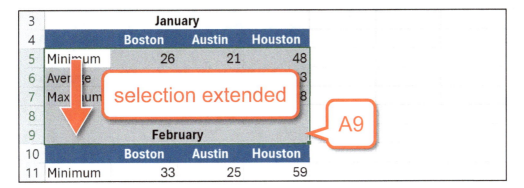

Result: By selecting the merged cell A9, the selection is automatically extended. As a result, it extends over the range from A5 to D9.

6. Select the cell range A5 to A19 and look at the result.

    Result: This selection is also automatically extended by the merged cells.

7. Select cell A9 and click on the **Merge & Center** button to remove the **Merge & Center** format.

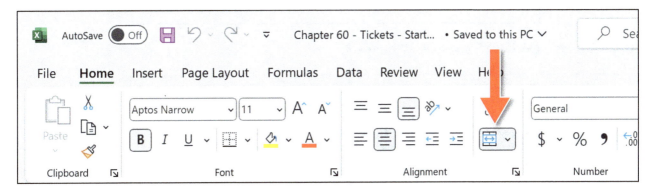

Result: The **Merge & Center** format is removed again. The text **February** is in cell A9. The cell range A9 to D9 is selected.

8. Click on the small arrow in the **Alignment** group.

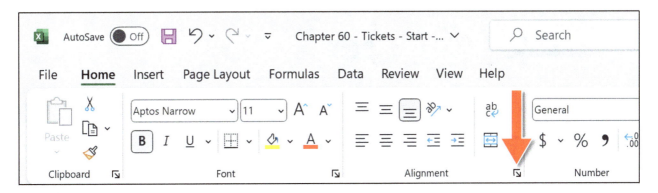

Result: The **Formal Cells** dialog box opens. As you click on the arrow in the **Alignment** group, the dialog box also opens with the **Alignment** tab.

9. Open the *Horizontal* list box and click on the *Center Across Selection* list item.

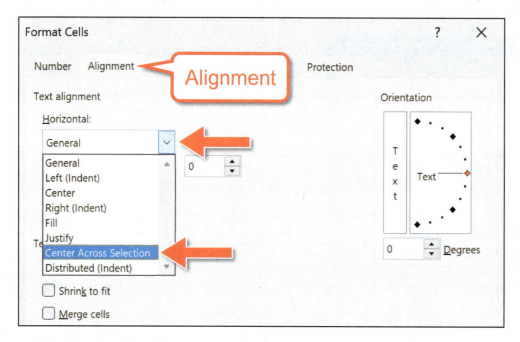

10. Click on the *OK* button and look at the result.

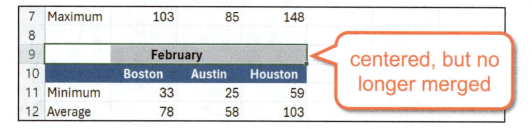

Result: A9 to D9 are no longer merged. However, the February heading is still centered.

11. Select cell A9 to better recognize that the connection has been removed.

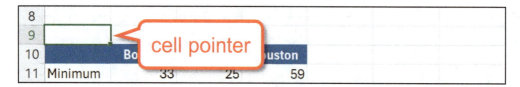

Result: By clicking on A9, the cell pointer is placed in this cell. However, it is only on A9 and no longer extends over the cell range from A9 to D9.

12. Also select A15 for comparison. A15 is still connected to cells B15, C15 and D15.

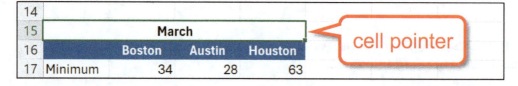

13. Remove the *Merge & Center* format for A3 and A15 as well and assign the *Center Across Selection* format.

14. Select the cell range A5 to A19 and set format to bold.

15. Save the file and close Excel.

61   Recovering unsaved workbooks

Sometimes people forget to save data. In some cases, Excel automatically creates backup copies. These instructions describe how you can access these backups.

Instruction

1. Open Excel and click on the *File* tab → *Open* → *Recover unsaved Workbooks* button.

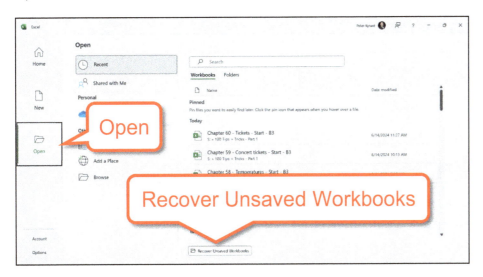

Result: The *Open* dialog box with unsaved workbooks is displayed.
Advice: If the *Recover Unsaved Workbooks* button is not visible, you do not currently have any unsaved workbooks. Excel files are also called worksheets or workbooks.

2. Look at the result.

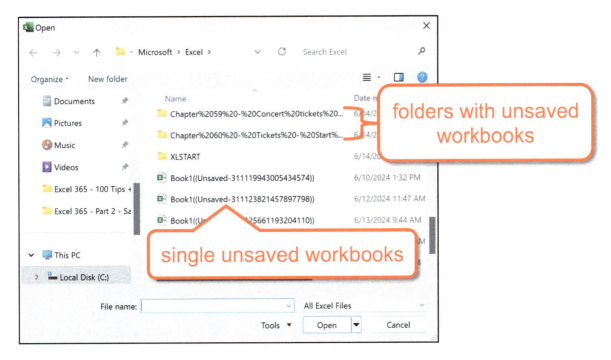

Advice: There are other unsaved files within the folders.
3. Open a folder or a single unsaved workbook by double-clicking it.
4. Edit the file and save the changes. Close Excel after you are done.

62   Hiding spreadsheets

Sometimes workbooks contain many spreadsheets, but only a few of them are currently being used. In these cases, it can be useful to hide spreadsheets. They are then no longer displayed as table tabs at the bottom of the screen and can be shown again at any time.

Instruction

1. Open the sample file: ***Chapter 62 - Shift schedule - Start - B3***
2. Right-click on the ***Week 21*** sheet tab.

Advice: Obsolete spreadsheets should be hidden for a better overview.

3. Click on the ***Hide*** button to hide the spreadsheet.

Result: The spreadsheet is hidden. Only ***Week 22*** and ***Week 20*** are displayed.

4. Repeat the process with the ***Week 20*** spreadsheet.

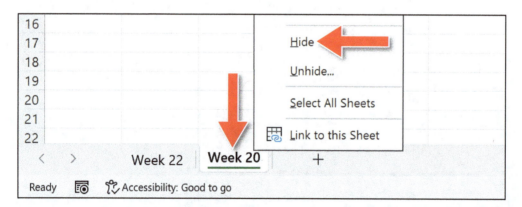

Advice: At least one sheet is always shown (visible). To show hidden tables again, right-click on a sheet tab → ***Unhide***. The Unhide dialog box appears. Select the sheet that you want to see again and confirm with the ***OK*** button.

5. Save the file and close Excel.

63   Inserting hyperlinks

These instructions describe how you can insert a link to another spreadsheet. When you click on the link, the other sheet is displayed.

Instruction

1. Open the sample file: ***Chapter 63 - Annual revenue - Start - B3***
2. Right-click on cell A4 to open the context menu.

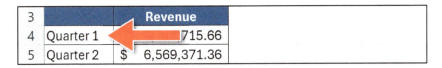

3. Click on the ***Link*** menu item to open the ***Insert Hyperlink*** dialog box.

4. Click on the ***Place in This Document*** button.

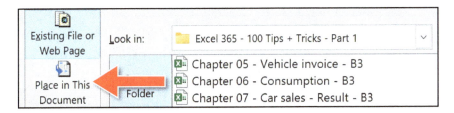

5. Click on ***Quarter1*** and confirm the entry with the ***OK*** button.

6. Look at the result. The content of the cell is displayed as a ***hyperlink*** (blue and underlined).

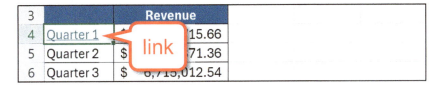

7. Click on the link to open the sheet tab ***Quarter1***.
   Advice: When pointing to this cell, the mouse is displayed as a hand 🖑 . You can return to your previous position by using the key combination ⌐Alt⌐ + ***left arrow key*** ⌐←⌐.
8. Create links for the remaining quarters.
   Advice: To edit the content of these cells, use the arrow keys to navigate and press ⌐F2⌐ to activate edit mode. You can also delete links by right-clicking the cell and clicking on ***Remove Hyperlink***.
9. Save the file and close Excel.

64   Fill function 1 - Creating a series of numbers quickly

These instructions describe how you can quickly create a simple series of numbers.

Instruction

1. Open Excel with an empty workbook.
2. Enter the number 1 in **A1**. However, do <u>not</u> press the **enter key** ⏎ yet.

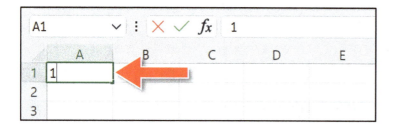

3. Position the mouse pointer on the fill handle (green square at the bottom right of the cell pointer).

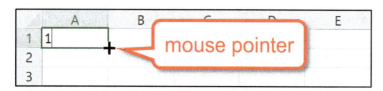

Result: The mouse pointer is displayed as a black cross **+**.

4. Press and hold the **control key** Ctrl .

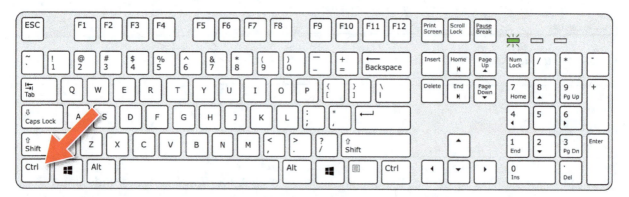

5. Hold down the left mouse button and drag the mouse to row 10 to create a series of numbers from 1 to 10.
6. Release the **control key** Ctrl and look at the result.

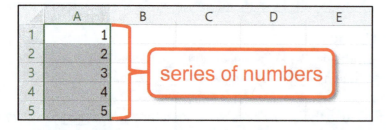

Result: The edit mode of cell A1 is ended and a series of numbers is generated.

7. Close Excel without saving.

65   Fill function 2 - Creating long series of numbers

These instructions describe how you can insert series of numbers of any size in columns or rows.

Instruction

1. Open Excel with an empty workbook.
2. Enter the number *1* in A1. Confirm the entry with the **enter key** ⏎ and select A1 again.
3. Click on the **Fill** button.

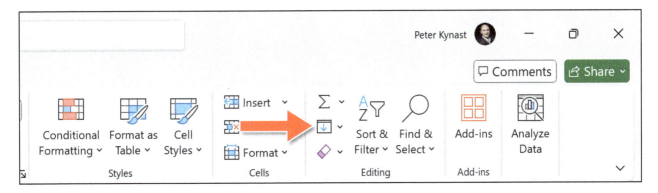

4. Click on the **Series** list item to open the **Series** dialog box.

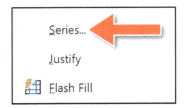

5. Activate the option **Columns** and enter 1000 in the **Stop value** field.

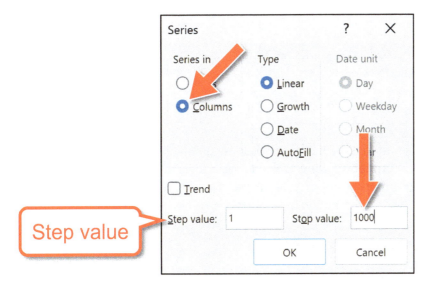

6. Confirm the dialog box with the **OK** button or by using the **enter key** ⏎.
   Result: The numbers 1 to 1000 are inserted in A1 to A1000.
   Advice: The step value specifies the value by which the next number should be increased.
7. Close Excel without saving.

66   Fill function 3 - Texts with numbers

These instructions describe how cell contents behave when they are filled in if they consist of text and numbers.

Instruction

1. Open Excel with an empty workbook.
2. Enter the following texts in A1 and B1.

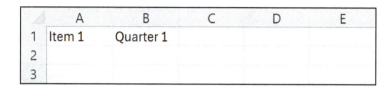

3. Select the cells A1 to B1 point the mouse on the fill handle (green square at the bottom right of the cell pointer).

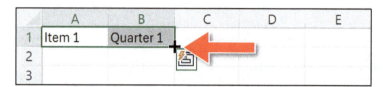

Result: The mouse pointer is displayed as a black cross ✚.

4. Click on the fill handle and drag the mouse to cell B6 while holding down the left mouse button.
5. Undo the selection and look at the result.

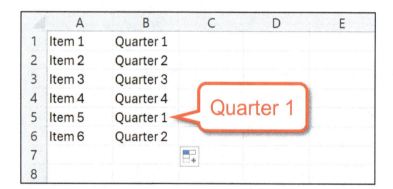

Result: Texts with numbers are automatically numbered consecutively (item 1, item 2, etc.). The term *quarter* is an exception. The numbering continues with quarter 1 after reaching quarter 4.
Advice: You can also try out different spellings, e.g.: 1 article, 1st article, article1, 1 quarter, 1st quarter, etc. With most spellings, a consecutive numbering is generated as shown. To deactivate consecutive numbering, press and hold down the ***control key*** [Ctrl] while dragging with the black cross ✚

6. Close Excel without saving.

67   Fill function 4 - Creating a list of sequential dates

These instructions describe several options for creating a list of sequential dates.

Instruction

1. Open Excel with an empty workbook.
2. Enter the following data.

	A	B	C	D	E
1	1/1/2024	1/1/2024	1/1/2024		
2			1/3/2024		
3					
4					

3. Select A1 and point the mouse on the fill handle (green square at the bottom right of the cell pointer).

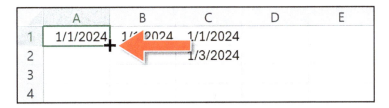

4. Click on the fill handle and drag the mouse to A5. Undo the selection and look at the result.

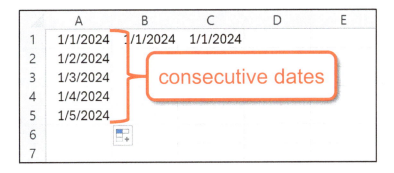

Result: The dates are continued.

5. Select cell B1 and keep the **_control key_** Ctrl held.

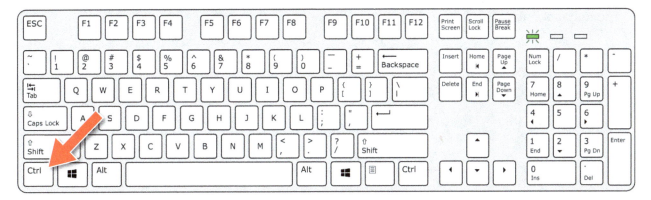

6. Click on the fill handle and drag the mouse to cell B5. Release the **control key** ☐Ctrl☐ and look at the result.

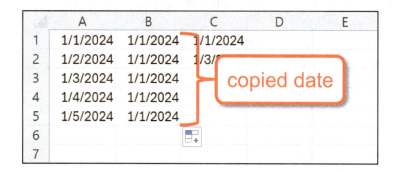

copied date

7. Select the cells C1 to C2 and position the mouse pointer on the fill handle.

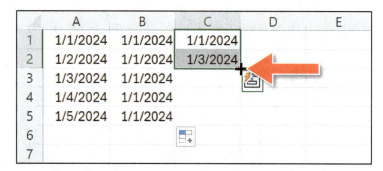

8. Hold down the mouse button and drag the mouse to cell C5. Look at the result.

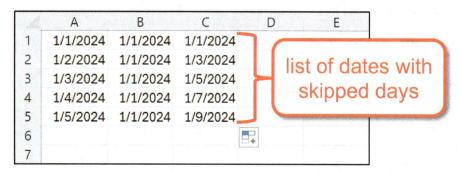

list of dates with skipped days

Advice: By selecting 2 dates, you can create a list of sequential dates with intervals. You can proceed in the same way with times. If you select 08:00 and 10:00 and drag with the black cross, you will get a series with an interval of 2 hours.

9. Close Excel without saving.

68   Fill function 5 - List of sequential dates without weekends

These instructions describe how you can create a list of sequential dates without weekends.

Instruction

1. Open Excel with an empty workbook.
2. Enter the date *1/1/2024* in cell A1. Select cell A1 and point to the fill handle (green square at the bottom right of the cell pointer).

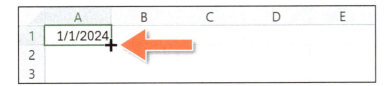

Result: The mouse pointer is displayed as a black cross **+**.

3. Click on the fill handle and drag the mouse to cell A31 while holding down the mouse button.

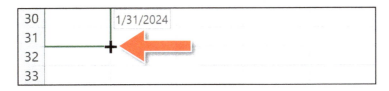

4. Click on the **Auto Fill Options** and select **Fill Weekdays**.

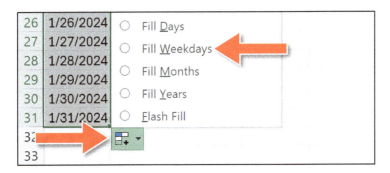

Result: The Saturdays and Sundays are removed from the date list. However, the list still extends to row 31. The removed days add days from the month of February. Public holidays are not considered with this method!

5. Look at the result.

Result: The weekends are removed from the list.

6. Close Excel without saving.

69   Fill function 6 - Custom lists

These instructions describe how you can create your own lists for the fill function. These lists are saved in Excel's basic settings and can then be used in any Excel file.

Instruction

1. Open the sample file: ***Chapter 69 - Employee list - B3***
2. Select the cell range A4 to A22.
   Advice: These names should be saved as a separate list.
3. Click on the ***File*** tab open the ***Backstage view***.
4. Click on the ***Options*** button at the bottom left of the backstage view.
   Attention: On smaller screens, you must first click on the ***More*** button and then on ***Options***.
5. In the ***Excel Options*** dialog box, click on the ***Advanced*** category and scroll to the bottom of this category. The scroll bar must start at the bottom. Then click on ***Edit Custom Lists***.

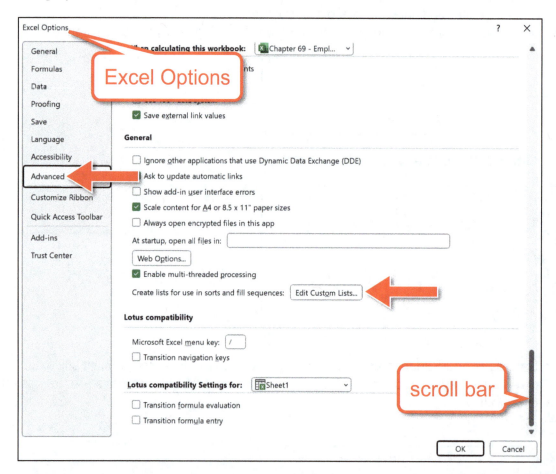

Result: The ***Custom Lists*** dialog box is displayed.

6. In the ***Custom Lists*** dialog box, click on the ***Import*** button to import the selected names.

Result: As you have previously selected the area with the names, it is already entered here.

7. Look at the result.

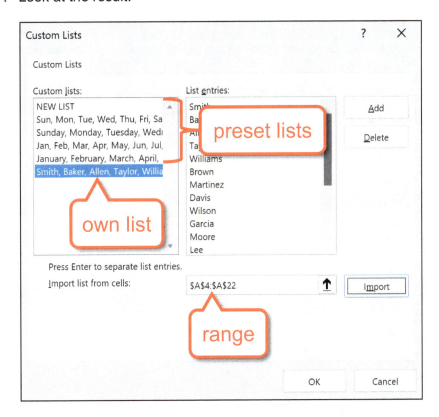

Result: By importing, the names are added as a custom list.

8. Click on the **OK** button to close the dialog box and save the new list in Excel's basic settings.
9. Close the **Excel Options** windows with the **OK** or **Cancel** button.
10. Close Excel without saving.
    Advice: As the list is saved in Excel's basic settings, you do <u>not</u> need to save the file.
11. Open Excel with any file or an empty workbook.
12. Enter <u>any</u> name from the list in a cell. Confirm the entry and select the cell.
13. Position your mouse on the fill handle (green square at the bottom right of the cell pointer).

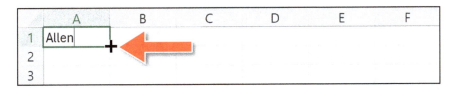

Result: The mouse pointer is displayed as a black cross **✚**.

14. Hold down the left mouse button and drag the mouse down or to the right to create a list of your own names.

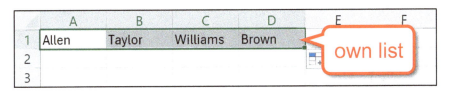

Result: The cells are filled in automatically. As soon as the first specified name is reached, the list starts from the beginning. You can use any text to start the list.

15. Close Excel without saving.

70   Fill function 7 - Copying formats only

These instructions describe how you can copy only the formats using the fill function.

Instruction

1. Open the sample file: ***Chapter 70 - Wages - Start - B3***
2. Select the area A6 to C7 and point to the fill handle with the mouse.

5	Name	Hours	Wage
6	**Jones**	165	$ 3,300.00
7	**Lopez**	186	$ 3,720.00
8	Brown	201	$ 4,020.00
9	Williams	130	$ 2,600.00

Advice: The mouse pointer is displayed as a black cross ✚.

3. Press and hold down the left mouse button and drag to row 15 to copy the cells.

13	**Lopez**	312	$ 6,240.00
14	**Jones**	333	$ 6,660.00
15	**Lopez**	354	$ 7,080.00
16		**2595**	**$51,900.00**
17			

Result: The formats are copied, but the data is also overwritten.

4. Click on the ***Auto Fill Options*** button to open the list box.

14	**Jones**	333	$ 6,660.00
15	**Lopez**	354	$ 7,080.00
16		**2595**	**$51,900.00**
17			

5. Click on the ***Fill Formatting Only***.

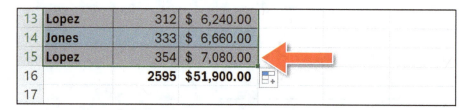

○ Copy Cells
◉ Fill Series
○ Fill Formatting Only
○ Fill Without Formatting

Result: The overwritten table data is restored. Only the formats of the first two table rows are copied to the rest of the tab.

6. Check the data.

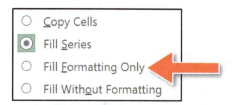

14	**Cruz**	69	$ 1,380.00
15	**Myers**	174	$ 3,480.00
16		**1449**	**$28,980.00**	sum
17			

7. Save the file and close Excel.

71 Showing and hiding rows and columns

These instructions describe how you can quickly show and hide rows and columns.

Instruction

1. Open the sample file: ***Chapter 71 - Customer visits - Start - B3***
2. Select any cell in row 6.
3. Press the key combination ***control key*** Ctrl + 9 to hide this row.

4. Look at the result. The line is hidden. The dividing line between 5 and 7 is thicker.

4	Davis	71	102	66
5	Rodriguez		3	114
7	Hernandez		1	94
8	Lopez	59	112	119

thicker dividing line → **hidden**

5. Select C11 to C21 and hide them using the same key combination.

9	Clark	91	64	
10	Gonzalez	92	86	**hidden**
22	Harris	96	89	
23	Johnson	88	51	56

Advice: It is not important in which column you select to hide. In this situation, you could also select A11 to A21 or E11 to E21.

6. Select the cells A5 to A7 or B5 to B7.

4	Davis	71	102	66
5	Rodriguez	113	93	114
7	Hernandez	120	101	94
8	Lopez	59	112	119

7. Press the key combination ***control key*** Ctrl + ***shift key*** ⇧ + 9 to show row 6 again.
   Advice: Columns are hidden with the key combination ***control key*** Ctrl + 0 . With the key combination ***control key*** Ctrl + ***shift key*** ⇧ + 0 you can show the columns again. Please note that you must first set a selection. The selection must contain and enclose the columns from both sides.
8. Save the file and close Excel.

72   Copying only visible cells

Rows or columns that are hidden are still copied. These instructions describe how you can copy only the visible cells.

Instruction

1. Open the sample file: ***Chapter 72 - Customer visits - Intermediate result - B3***
2. Place the cell pointer in the cell range A1 to D24.
3. Press the key combination ***control key*** `Ctrl` + `A` to select the entire area.
4. Click on the ***Find & Select*** button in the ***Home*** tab.

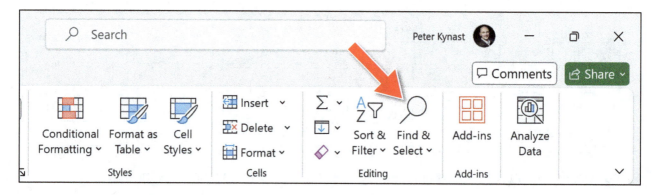

5. Click on the ***Go To Special*** list item.

6. Activate the ***Visible cells only*** option.

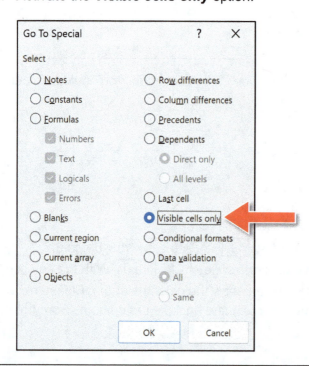

7. Confirm the setting with the **OK** button.
    Result: The selection is reduced in size. Only the visible cells are selected.
8. Click on the **Copy** button in the **Home** tab.
9. Click on the plus sign at the bottom of the Excel window to insert a new sheet.

10. Click on the **Paste** button in the **Home** tab to insert the data in new sheet.
11. Look at the result.

	A	B	C	D	E	F
1	Name	January	February	March		
2	Garcia	92	81	88		
3	Miller	103	106	75		
4	Davis	71	102	66		
5	Rodriguez	113	93	114		
6	Martinez	60	51	75		
7	Hernandez	120	101	94		
8	Lopez	59	112	119		
9	Clark	91	64	85		
10	Gonzalez	92	86	72		
11	Harris	96	89	71		
12	Johnson	88	51	56		
13	Williams	96	100	103		
14				(Ctrl) ▾		
15						

Result: Only the visible rows were copied and pasted.
Attention: If you have set filters in a data area and copy filtered data, only the visible data is copied by default. In this case, it is not necessary to use **Go To Special → Visible cells** only.

12. Save the file and close Excel.

73 Calculating the total using a key combination

These instructions describe how you can create the sum of a range using a key combination.

Instruction

1. Open the sample file: **Chapter 73 - Heating oil - Start - B3**
2. Select the cell range D6 to D15.

	Date	Quantity ordered in gallons	Cost per gallon	Total
3		Orders since 2014		
4				
5	**Date**	**Quantity ordered in gallons**	**Cost per gallon**	**Total**
6	1/31/2014	214	$ 2.69	$ 575.66
7	3/18/2015	217	$ 1.54	$ 334.18
8	3/18/2016	274	$ 1.29	$ 353.46
9	4/9/2017	305	$ 1.58	$ 481.90
10	4/22/2018	258	$ 2.06	$ 531.48
11	5/21/2019	212	$ 1.92	$ 407.04
12	6/5/2020	233	$ 1.20	$ 279.60
13	8/25/2021	268	$ 1.91	$ 511.88
14	12/17/2022	229	$ 3.57	$ 817.53
15	12/1/2023	172	$ 2.68	$ 460.96
16				

3. Press the key combination ⎡Alt⎤ + *equal sign key* ⎡=⎤.

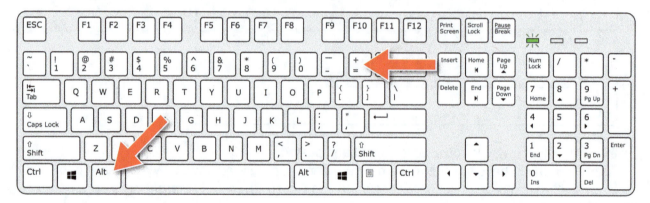

4. Look at the result.

	Date	Quantity ordered in gallons	Cost per gallon	Total
11	5/21/2019	212	$ 1.92	$ 407.04
12	6/5/2020	233	$ 1.20	$ 279.60
13	8/25/2021	268	$ 1.91	$ 511.88
14	12/17/2022	229	$ 3.57	$ 817.53
15	12/1/2023	172	$ 2.68	$ 460.96
16				$ 4,753.69	sum
17				
18				

5. Save the file and close Excel.

74   Moving cells with the mouse

These instructions describe how you can move cells.

Instruction

1. Open the sample file: ***Chapter 74 - Field service - Start - B3***
2. Select the cell range D2 to D6.

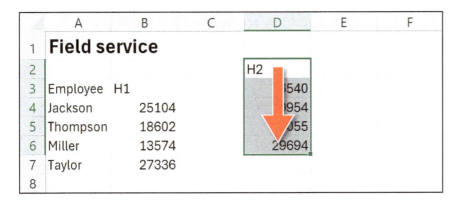

3. Use the mouse to point to the cell pointer (green edge of the selection).

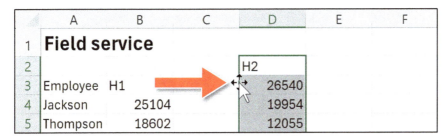

Result: The mouse pointer is displayed as a white arrow with 4 small black arrows.

4. Click on the edge of the cell pointer and drag the area to the range C3 to C7 while holding down the mouse button. However, do <u>not</u> click on the fill handle (green square at the bottom right of the cell pointer).

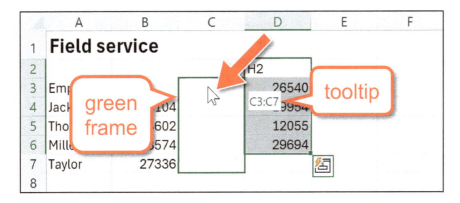

Result: The cells are moved. If the range contains formats, these are also moved.
Advice: The tooltip shows where the cells are moved to. In Excel, the colon is part of the range specification and means ***to***. In Excel, the colon <u>never</u> stands for ratios or odds!

5. Save the file and close Excel.

75   Copying cells quickly

These instructions describe how you can copy cells quickly. These can be individual cells or cell ranges. In the following example, the first half of a budget is to be copied. This copy is then to be filled with the data for the second half of the year. As only a small amount of data changes in the second half of the year, copying the first half of the year makes sense in this case.

Instruction

1. Open the sample file: *Chapter 75 - Housekeeping budget - Start - B3*
2. Click on any cell in the range from A3 to G11.
3. Press the key combination *control key* Ctrl + A to select this area.
4. Use the mouse to point to the cell pointer (green edge of the selection).

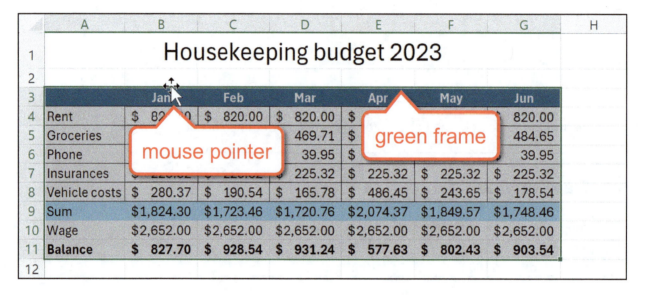

Result: The mouse is displayed as a white arrow with 4 small black arrows .

5. Press and hold the *control key* Ctrl .

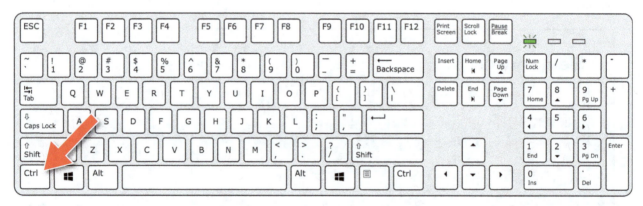

Advice: The control key now no longer moves content but copies it to the selected position.

6. Keep the **control key** `Ctrl` pressed and drag the copy of the table to the target area A13 to G21. Use the green frame as a guide.

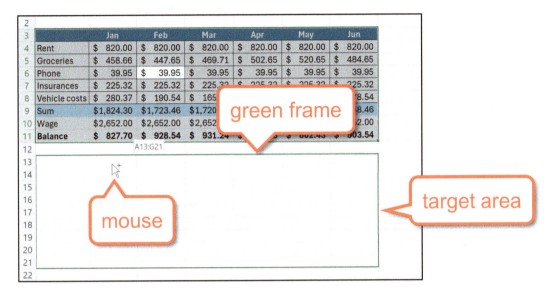

7. Release the mouse button and look at the result.

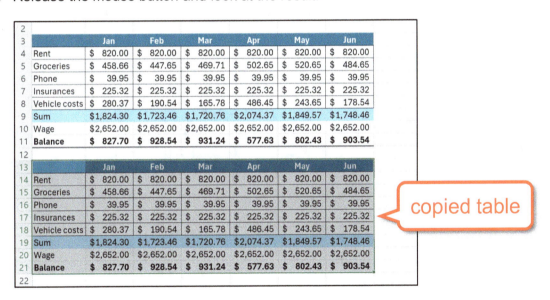

Result: A copy of the table is inserted. The month labels are still incorrect.

8. Enter the text *Jul* in B13. Complete the entry and select B13.

9. Place the mouse pointer on the fill handle and drag the mouse to G13 while holding down the mouse button to enter the months of the second half of the year.

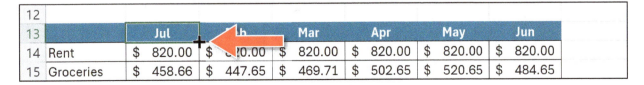

Result: The old months are overwritten.

Advice: When pointing to the fill handle, the mouse is displayed as a black cross ✚.

10. Save the file and close.

76   Remaining in the current cell after confirming the input

When confirming entries with the **enter key** ⏎ , Excel moves the cell pointer down one cell. In some cases, this behavior is not useful, e.g. because the fill function is to be used directly afterwards to create a list or a format is assigned. These instructions describe how to remain in the same cell when confirming an entry.

Instruction

1. Open Excel with an empty workbook.
2. Enter the word **January** in any cell. Do <u>not</u> complete the entry yet!

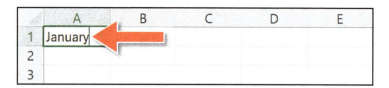

3. Press the key combination **control key** Ctrl + **enter key** ⏎ to complete the entry.

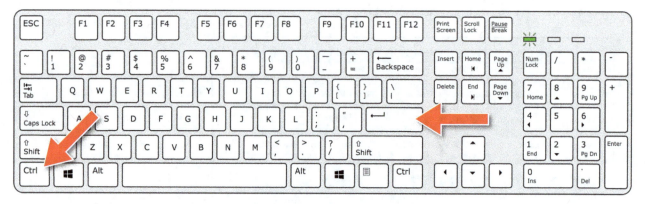

4. Look at the result. The cell pointer remains on the same cell after the entry.

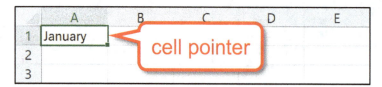

cell pointer

5. Place the mouse on the fill handle and, holding down the left mouse button, drag the mouse to row 12 to create a list of the months January to December.

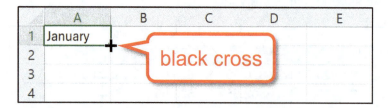

black cross

Advice: When you place the mouse on the fill handle (green square at the bottom right of the cell pointer), the mouse pointer is displayed as a black cross ✚.

6. Close Excel without saving.

77   Inserting calculated content

These instructions describe how you can apply a calculation to several existing figures. The sales projection values in this table should be increased by a factor of 1.5.

Instruction

1. Open the sample file: ***Chapter 77 - Hardware store - Start - B3***
2. Enter the value ***1.5*** in D4. Complete the entry with the key combination ***control key*** ⏎Ctrl + ***enter key*** ⏎ so that the cell pointer remains on D4 after the entry is completed.

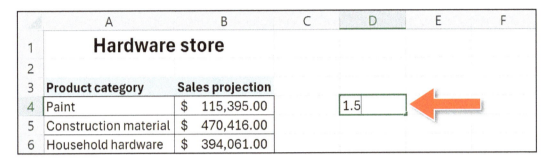

Advice: If you only complete the entry with the enter key, the cell pointer is set to D5. You must first select cell D4 again.

3. Click on the ***Copy*** 🗋 to copy the value.

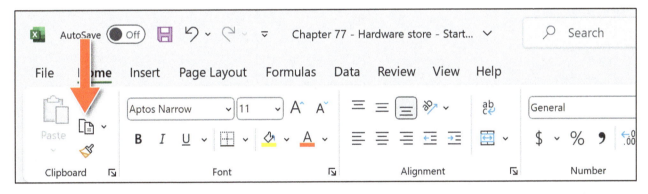

4. Select the cell range B4 to B10.
   Advice: The numbers in this area should be multiplied by 1.5.
5. Click on the small arrow under the ***Paste*** button.

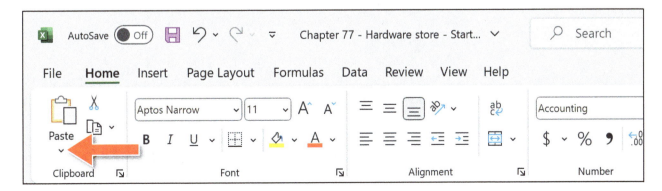

6. Click on the **Paste Special** button to open the **Paste Special** dialog box.

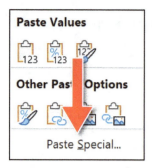

7. Click on the **Values** and **Multiply** options. Confirm the settings with the **OK** button or the **enter key** ⏎.

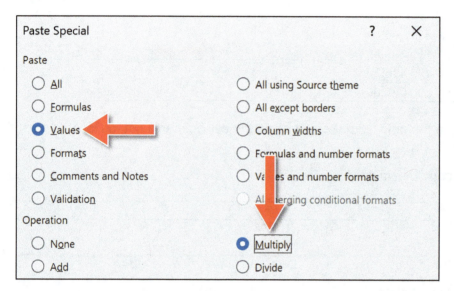

Advice: With the setting **Paste → All**, the formats of the target area would also be overwritten. The **Values** setting only offsets the numbers against the copied value.

8. Look at the result.

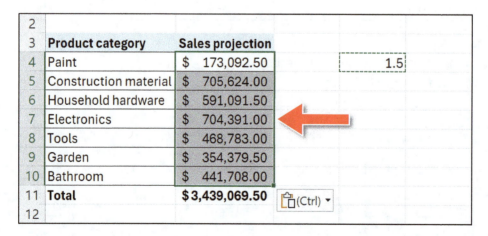

Result: The selected cell range B4 to B10 is multiplied by a factor of **1.5**. The dollar format is retained as only values have been inserted. The total is automatically recalculated.

9. Delete the value in D4.
10. Save the file and close Excel.

78   Adjusting table size to a page with letter format

These instructions describe how you can adapt a table to a single page in the US Letter format.

Instruction

1. Open the sample file: ***Chapter 78 - Meal order - Start - B3***
2. Look at the table. It contains 20 rows for food orders and should be printed on a single page. Scroll down to see the last row (20).
3. Click on the ***File*** tab to open the ***Backstage view***.

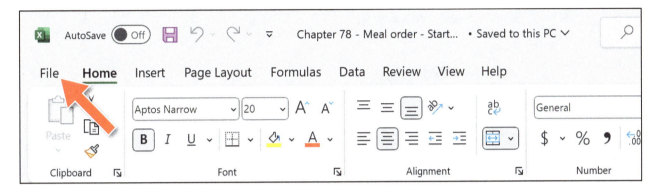

Advice: If you click on the File tab, the so-called Backstage view is always opened. This is the official name of this page. Here you have access to important Excel functions, e.g. printing, opening and saving files. You will also find templates, the options (basic Excel settings) and your Microsoft account details here.

4. Click on the ***Print*** category and look at the result.

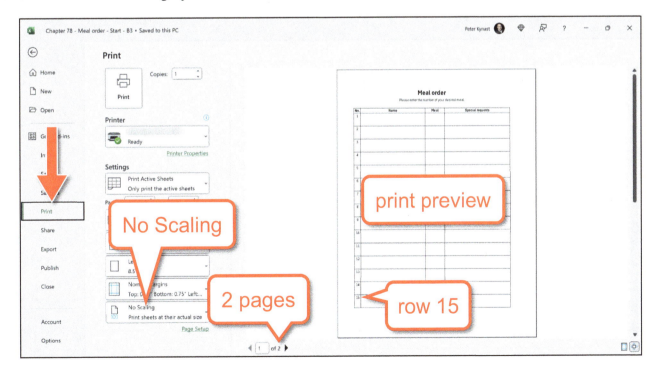

Advice: The term scaling stands for the enlargement or reduction of the table during printing. By default, tables are printed in their original size (without scaling).

5. Click on the **No Scaling** and then on **Fit Sheet on One Page**.

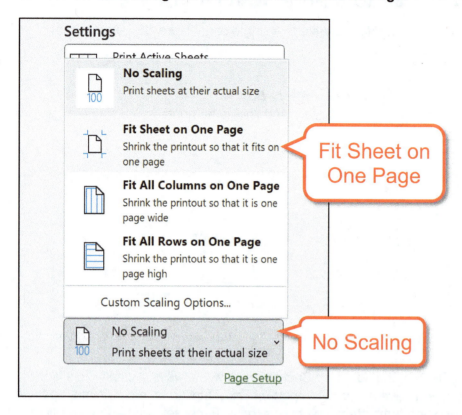

Result: The setting **Fit Sheet on One Page** shrinks the table so that it fits on a single page.

6. Look at the result.

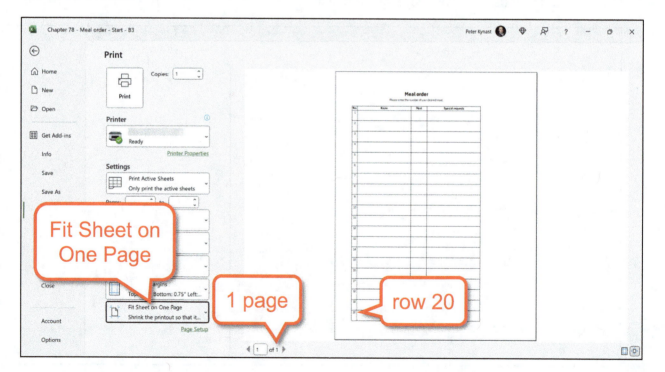

Result: The table is reduced in size and fits on one page. All 20 rows are visible.

7. Save the file and close Excel.

Advice: Printing settings like scaling, paper type and orientation are saved to the current document.

79   Print title

These instructions describe how you can repeat the top row(s) of a table on each page of the printout.

Instruction

1. Open the sample file: *Chapter 79 - Trip - Start - B3*
2. Click on the *Print Titles* button in the *Page Layout* tab to open the *Page Setup* dialog box.

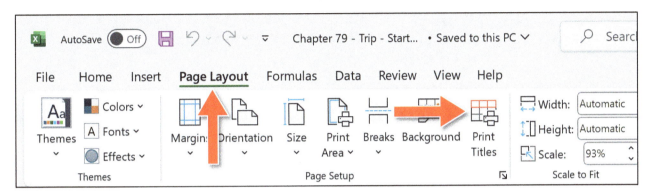

3. Click on the *Rows to repeat at top* field to place the cursor there.

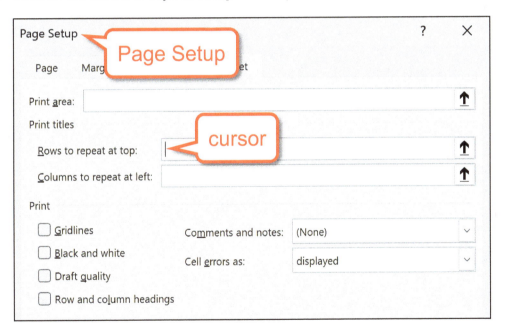

4. Click on row 1 in the spreadsheet and drag the mouse down to row 3 to select the first 3 rows.

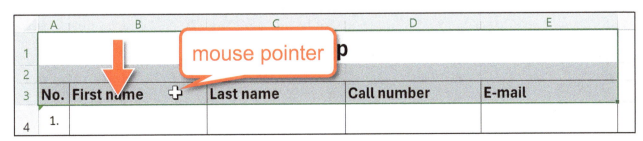

Result: The *Page Setup* window is temporarily reduced to just the *Rows to Repeat at top* input field while dragging the mouse.

5. Release the mouse button and look at the result.

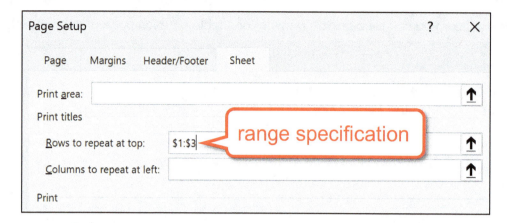

Result: The range specification *$1:$3* is displayed in the **Rows to repeat at top** field. This means that rows 1 to 3 are selected and will be repeated on the printout of each page.

6. Confirm the setting with the **OK** button.
7. Click on the **File** tab → **Print** to open the printing dialog.
8. Click on the right arrow at the bottom to display the next page. Look at the result.

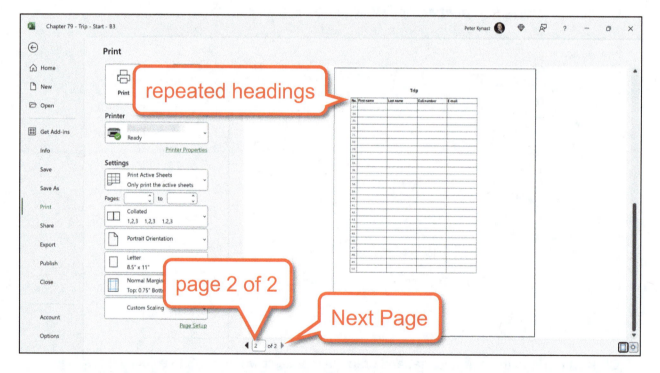

Result: The first 3 lines with the headings are repeated on the second page. However, the number of rows per page is currently still unequal and must be corrected. The next chapter describes this process. There should be 25 lines for names on each page.

9. Save the file and close Excel.

80   Setting page breaks

When printing tables, the page break is not always in the desired position. These instructions describe how you can change the page break of a table for the printout.

Instruction

1. Open the sample file: ***Chapter 80 - Trip - Intermediate result - B3***
2. Click on the ***Page Break Preview*** button in the ***View*** tab.

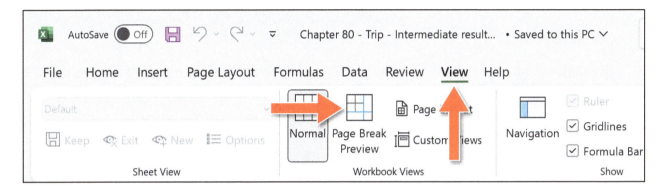

3. Point the mouse to the blue line and keep the mouse button pressed.

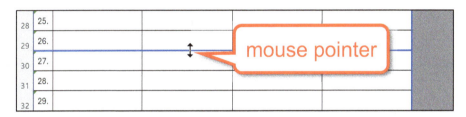

Advice: The blue line symbolizes the current page break.
Attention: Depending on your monitor, the blue line might be displayed thinner and dashed instead of a thicker blue line.

4. Drag the mouse between lines 25 and 26.

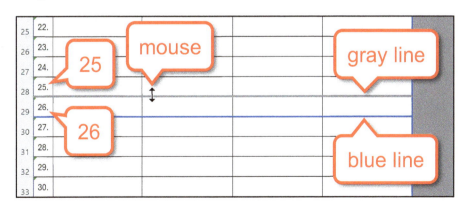

Attention: These two values refer to the numbers entered in column A. You can also use the row numbers as a guide. In this case, draw the line between rows 28 and 29.

5. Click on the **Normal** button in the **View** tab to exit the page break preview.

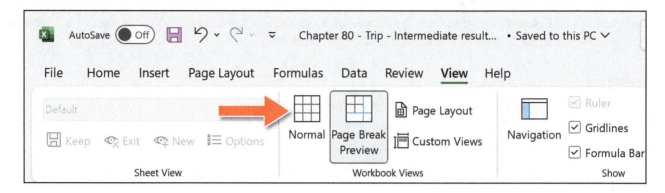

Advice: The entire table is not displayed in the wrap preview. You should therefore return to the normal view after changing the break points.

6. Click on the **File** Tab → **Print** and check the print preview.

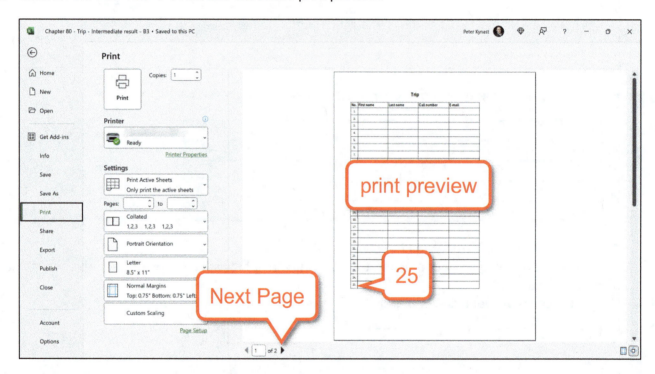

Result: The numbering ends at 25 on the first page. 25 numbered lines are displayed on both pages.

7. Display the second page by clicking on the arrow and check the numbering.
8. Save the file and close Excel.

81   Print area

With a print area, you define which area of a table is printed. In the following example, there is an explanatory note next to the actual table. This note should never be printed.

Instruction

1. Open the sample file: ***Chapter 81 - Class schedule - Start - B3***
2. Select the cell area from A1 to F12.
   Advice: Only this area should appear on the printout.
3. Click on the ***Print Area*** button in the ***Page Layout*** tab.

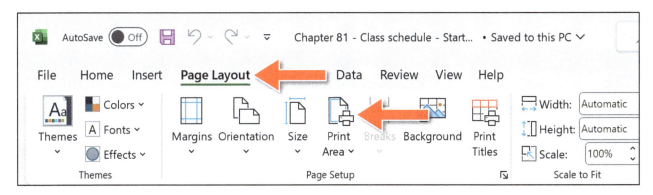

4. Click on the ***Set Print Area*** list item.

5. Click on the ***File*** tab → ***Print***. Look at the result.

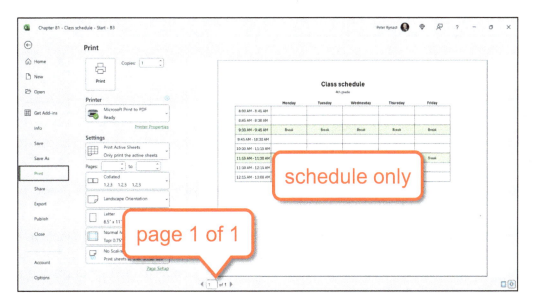

Result: Only the schedule is printed. No other page exists.
Advice: If you want to clear a print area again. Click on ***Print Area*** → ***Clear Print Area*** in the ***Page Layout*** tab.
6. Save the file and close Excel.

82   Group mode 1

If you want to carry out the same process in all sheets in a workbook, e.g. entering content in cells or applying formats, you can use group mode for this.

Instruction

1. Open the sample file: ***Chapter 82 - Supermarket - Start - B3***
2. Click on several sheet tabs and look at the content of the tables.
    Result: All tables have the same structure and identical contents. Only the name of the city in A1 differs on the sheet tabs.
3. Right-click on any sheet tab and then click on ***Select All Sheets*** to activate group mode.

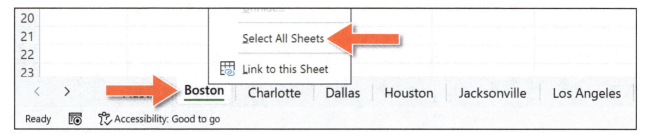

4. Look at the result.

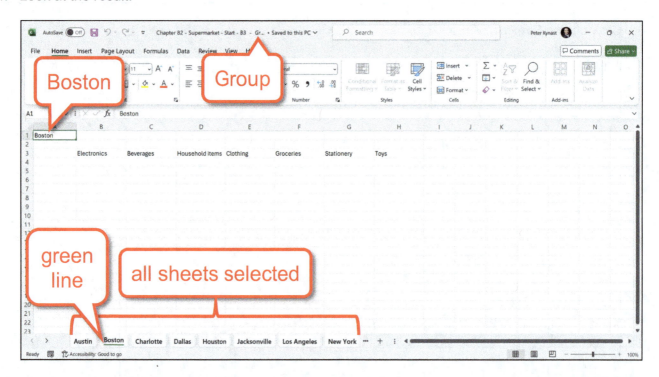

Result: All table tabs are displayed in white. The sheet tab that you right-clicked on is displayed. It is the active sheet tab. The name of this tab is underlined with a green line. In the title bar of Excel, the addition ***Group*** is displayed behind the file name. The addition ***Group*** might be cut off due to monitor size and display resolution settings.

5. Make the following changes:
    *   Format the heading in A1 with font size 16 and bold.
    *   Fill the area from A4 to A15 with the months January to December.
    *   Format the area A3 to H15 with all borders.

- Format A4 to A15 and B3 to H3 in bold.
- Set a light blue fill color for A3 to H3.
- Center the cell range B3 to H3.

6. Click on any sheet tab to deactivate group mode again. However do <u>not</u> click on the active sheet tab.

Attention: If you click on the active sheet tab, no change will occur. All tables remain selected in this case. Pay attention to the color of the sheet tabs.

7. Look at the result.

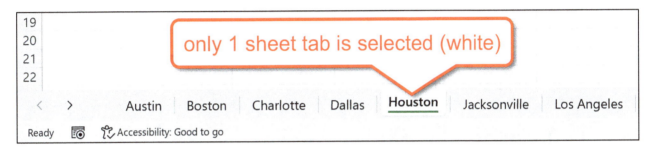

Result: Only one table tab is displayed in white. Group mode is no longer active. The **Group** addition is no longer displayed in the Excel title bar.

8. Click on various sheet tabs and check all tables.

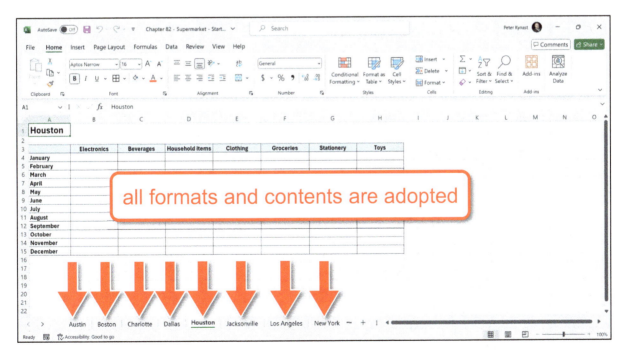

Result: The formats and contents were copied to all tables.

9. Save the file and close Excel.

83   Group mode 2

These instructions describe how you can select multiple sheet tabs at once.

Instruction

1. Open the sample file: ***Chapter 83 - Fruits - Start - B3***
2. Click on all sheet tabs and look at the contents of the tables.
    Result: The tables are structured differently and have different contents.
    Advice: The sheet tabs Quarter 2 and 4 should be matched with Quarters 1 and 3.
3. Click on the sheet tab for ***Quarter 2*** to activate it.

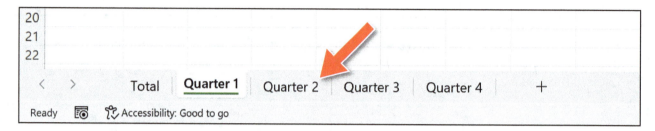

4. Press and hold the ***control key*** ⎵Ctrl⎵. Click on the sheet tab for ***Quarter 4***.
5. Release the ***control key*** ⎵Ctrl⎵ again and look at the result.

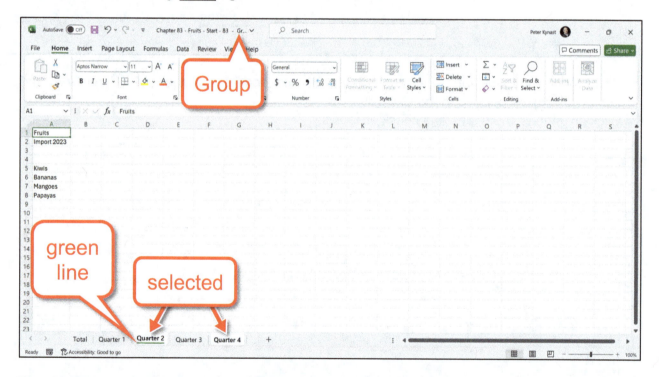

Result: The two sheet tabs are highlighted. The ***Quarter 2*** tab is the active sheet, which is why the Quarter 2 tab has a green line. The ***Group*** addition is displayed in the Excel title bar.
6. Make the following changes to the two tables:
    • Enter the word ***Amount*** in B4.
    • Format the heading in A1 in font size 16 and bold.
7. Click on a sheet tab that is <u>not</u> selected (Total, Quarter 1 or Quarter 3) to exit group mode again.
    Result: Only one sheet tab is displayed in white. The ***Group*** addition is no longer displayed.
8. Save the file and close Excel.

84 Group mode 3

These instructions describe how you can select several adjacent sheet tabs.

Instruction

1. Open the sample file: ***Chapter 84 - Cut flowers - Start - B3***
2. Click on every sheet tabs in turn and look at the contents of the tables.
   Result: The names of the flowers are missing in the tables for quarters 1 to 4.
3. Click on the sheet tab for ***Quarter 1*** to activate it.

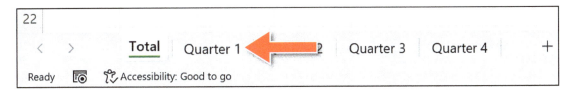

4. Press and hold the ***shift key*** ⬆. Click on the ***Quarter 4*** sheet tab.
5. Release the ***shift key*** ⬆ and look at the result.

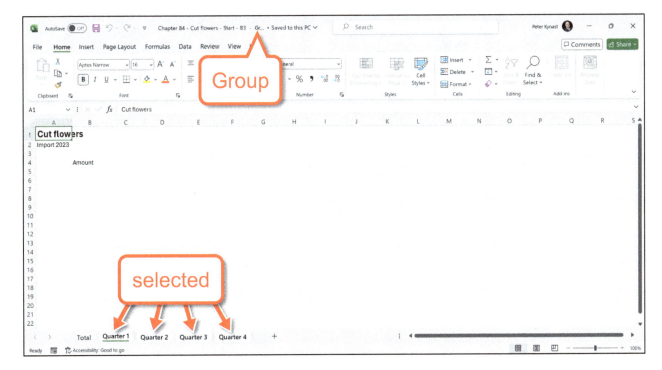

Result: The group mode is active. Quarters 1 to 4 are selected. They are displayed in white. The tab for quarter 1 has a green line. It is the active spreadsheet.
Advice: You can use the ***control key*** Ctrl to select several individual sheet tabs. Use the shift key to create a selection up to and including the tab that you clicked on.

6. Enter the terms ***Roses***, ***Tulips*** and ***Carnations*** in the range A5 to A7.
7. Click on the ***Total*** sheet tab to exit group mode again.
   Attention: The Total tab is the only tab that is not highlighted. If you were to click on a highlighted (white) tab (quarter 1, 2, 3 or 4), group mode would remain active.
8. Check the tables for quarters 1 to 4.
9. Save the file and close Excel.

85   Names 1

Names can make formulas easier to read and simplify processes. These instructions describe how you can create names for cells and use names in formulas.

Instruction

1. Open the sample file: ***Chapter 85 - Groceries - Start - B3***
2. Select cell B3 and click into the name field.

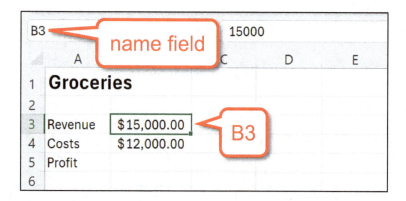

> **Advice:** The name field displays the name of the currently selected cell (B3).

3. Enter the term ***Revenue*** in the name field.

4. Confirm the entry with the ***enter key*** ⏎.
    Attention: Names <u>must</u> be confirmed by pressing the enter key. Otherwise the name will <u>not</u> be assigned.
5. Look at the result.

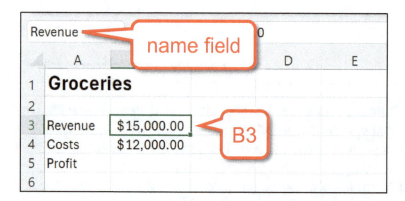

Result: The name field displays the term ***Revenue***.
Advice: B3 now has the <u>additional</u> name ***Revenue***. The cell can be addressed using this name in a formula. However, the old name B3 is still valid. If you have made a mistake when assigning a name, you can correct it in the ***Formulas*** tab → ***Name-Manager***.

6. Select cell B4 and enter the term **Costs**.

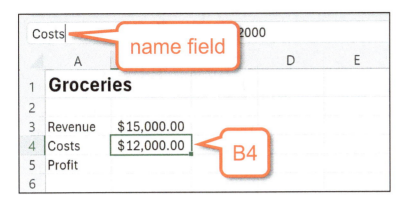

7. Confirm the entry with the **enter key** ⏎.
8. Select cell B5 and enter the formula **=Revenue-Costs**.

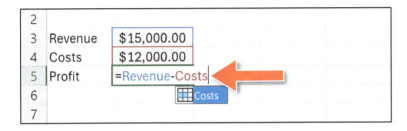

Result: The two names **Revenue** and **Costs** are highlighted in color.
Advice: The formula **=B3-B4** would also be valid and lead to the same result. By using the names, however, the formula is easier to understand.

9. Confirm the entry with the **enter key** ⏎.
10. Click on the arrow in the name field to open the list box.

Result: The names assigned in this table are displayed.
Advice: If you want to know whether there are names in a table, open the name field. It is particularly useful when working with external tables to check whether names have been used in the table.

11. Click on the name **Costs** to select this cell.

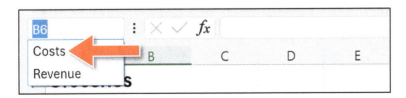

Result: The cell B4 (Costs) is selected.
Advice: By clicking on the name, you can find out which cell or cells this name has been assigned to. Cell ranges can also be assigned names.

12. Save the file and close Excel.

86   Names 2

These instructions describe how you can assign names to cell ranges and calculate with them.

Instruction

1. Open the sample file: **_Chapter 86 - Power consumption - Start - B3_**
2. Select the cell range B5 to B18.
3. Click into the name field and enter the name **_Consumption_**.

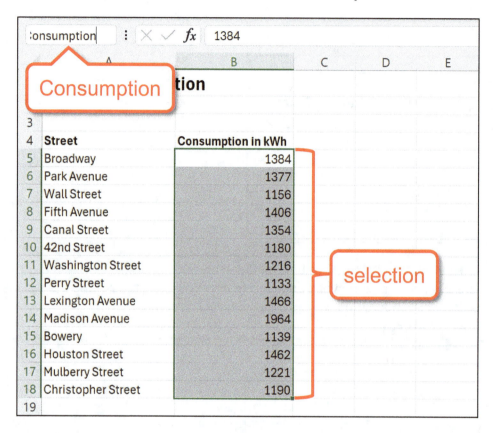

Advice: In the previous chapter, <u>single</u> cells were given names. In this example,, a name is assigned to <u>cell range</u>.

4. Confirm the entry with the **_enter key_** ⏎ .

    Attention: You <u>must</u> press the **_enter key_** ⏎ to confirm the entry. If you do not press enter after entering the name and click on the table instead, the name will not be assigned. Repeat the process in this case.
5. Enter the formula **_=SUM(Consumption)_** in cell B19 to add up the values.

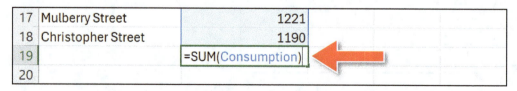

Advice: In this example, the name **_Consumption_** has been assigned to the cell range B5 to B18. It can replace the conventional range specification in a function.

6. Confirm the entry with the **_enter key_** ⏎ .
7. Save the file and close Excel.

87   Names 3

These instructions describe how you can correct incorrect names.

Instruction

1. Open the sample file: **Chapter 87 - Rent - Start - B3**
2. Open the list box of the name field and check the names contained in the table.

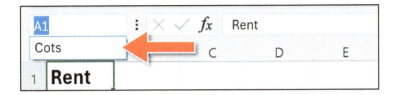

Result: The table contains only one name. The word **Costs** has been misspelled.

3. Click on the **Name Manager** button in the **Formulas** tab.

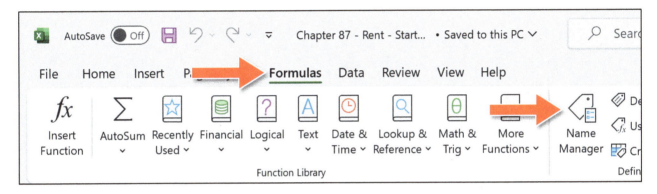

4. Look at the **Name Manager**.

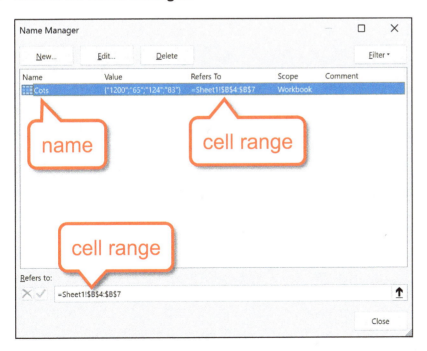

Advice: The Name Manager contains an overview of all existing names in this file. The corresponding cells or cell ranges are also displayed.

5. Click on the *Edit* button.

Result: The *Edit Name* window opens.

6. Correct the name to *Costs*.

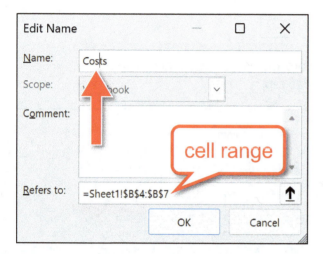

Advice: If required, you can also change the area to which the name refers in this window.

7. Confirm the change with the *OK* button.

Result: The name manager is displayed again. The name has been corrected.

8. Check the name.

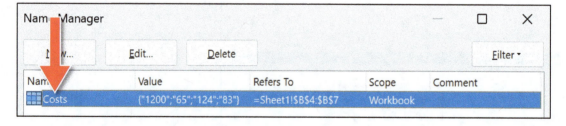

9. Click on the *Close* button to close the name manager.

10. Enter the formula *=SUM(Costs)* to add the values.

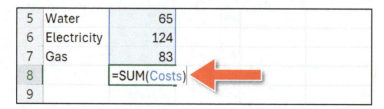

11. Confirm the entry with the *enter key* ⏎.

12. Save the file and close Excel.

88   Creating dynamic numbering

Numbering is often static. If rows are inserted, the series of numbers must be corrected or extended. Static numbering also does not adapt to sorting. These instructions describe how you can create dynamic numbering.

Instruction

1. Open the sample file: *Chapter 88 - Members - Start - B3*
2. Enter the formula *=ROW()* in cell A4.

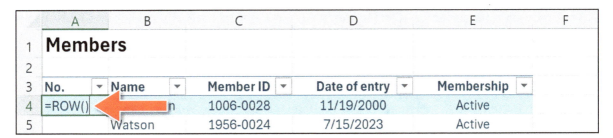

3. Confirm the entry and look at the result.

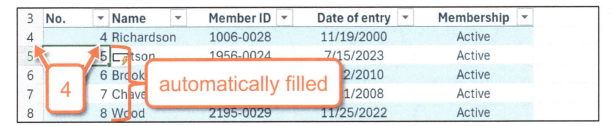

Result: The *=ROW()* function outputs the number of the row in which you enter the formula. As this is a smart table, the list is automatically filled to the end.

4. Change the formula in A4 to: *=ROW()-3*

Advice: The result in A4 should be the value 1, therefore the formula is *=ROW()-3*.

5. Confirm the entry and look at the result.

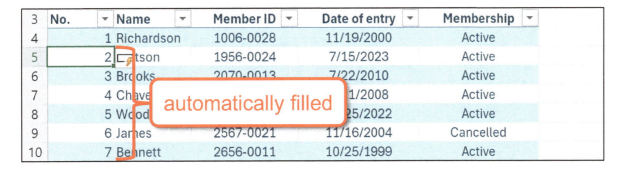

Result: The numbering starts with the value 1. The following values are filled automatically.

---

6. Press the key combination **control key** $\boxed{\text{Ctrl}}$ + **down arrow key** $\boxed{\downarrow}$ to place the cell pointer in cell A50.

7. Press the key combination **control key** $\boxed{\text{Ctrl}}$ + **shift key** $\boxed{\Uparrow}$ + **equal sign key** $\boxed{=}$ to add a new row to the smart table. Look at the result.

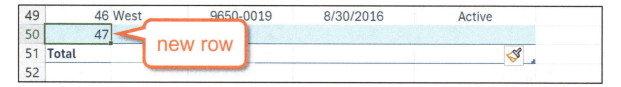

Result: A new row is inserted between number 46 and the total row. The numbering 47 appears automatically.

Advice: New rows are always inserted <u>above</u> the position of the cell pointer.

8. Click on the arrow in the **Name** heading to open the list box.

3	No. ▼	Name ▼	Member ID ▼	Date of entry ▼	Membership ▼
4	1	Richardson	1006-0028	11/19/2000	Active
5	2	Watson	1956-0024	7/15/2023	Active
6	3	Brooks	2070-0013	7/22/2010	Active
7	4	Chavez	2174-0013	4/21/2008	Active
8	5	Wood	2195-0029	11/25/2022	Active
9	6	James	2567-0021	11/16/2004	Cancelled

9. Click on the **Sort A to Z** list item to sort the list by name in ascending order.

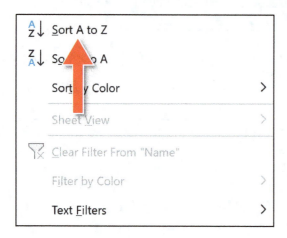

10. Look at the result.

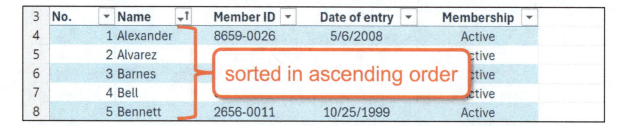

3	No. ▼	Name ▼↑	Member ID ▼	Date of entry ▼	Membership ▼
4	1	Alexander	8659-0026	5/6/2008	Active
5	2	Alvarez			ctive
6	3	Barnes			ctive
7	4	Bell			ctive
8	5	Bennett	2656-0011	10/25/1999	Active

Result: The names are sorted in ascending order. The numbering has <u>not</u> changed.

11. Save the file and close Excel.

89   Splitting tables

It is difficult to compare content in large lists. This is especially true if the values to be compared are far apart. This guide describes how you can split a large table to make it easier to compare such values.

In this example, a police officer examines phone connections. The aim is to find out whether the number (231) 298-7654 was called from the number (212) 583-4175 on two specific days. The two days are 7/11/2023 and 7/20/2023.

Instruction

1. Open the sample file: ***Chapter 89 - Phone connections - Start - B3***
2. Select the cell A117.
    Advice: The first phone call took place on 7/11/2023 (row 116). The split is always activated above and to the left of the position of the cell pointer.
3. Click on the **Split** button in the **View** tab to activate the splitting of the table.

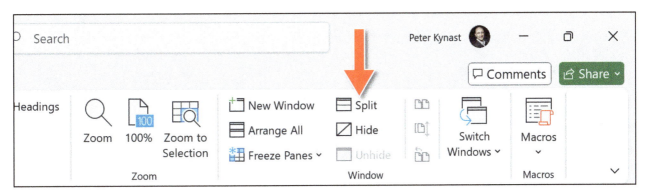

4. Look at the result.

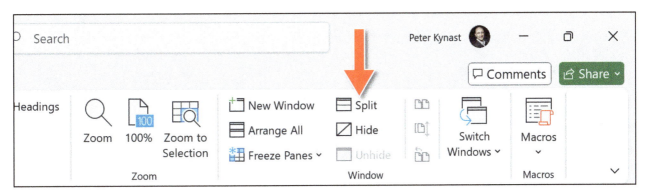

Result: The table is divided into 2 areas. The two areas can be scrolled separately from each other. The division is displayed as a gray line.

5. In the lower area, scroll to row 221. This row contains the telephone connection you are looking for.

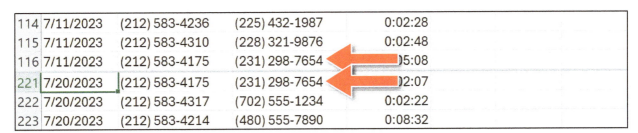

Advice: You can also use the ***up arrow key*** ⬆ and the ***down arrow key*** ⬇ to scroll the list in small steps. To scroll the other area, you must first place the cell pointer in this area.

6. Save the file and close Excel.

90   Linking cells 1

At the end of a long table is a result. It is based on a longer formula. You want to be able to see the result at the top of the table and save yourself having to re-enter the long formula. These instructions describe how you can link a cell to the result cell.

Instruction

1. Open the sample file: ***Chapter 90 - Smallest value - Start - B3***
2. Select cell D4 and enter an equal sign (=).

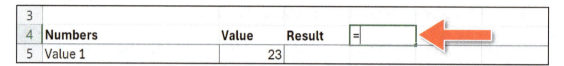

Advice: The result should be displayed a second time in this cell.
3. Click on cell B77 to insert the cell reference of this cell into the formula.

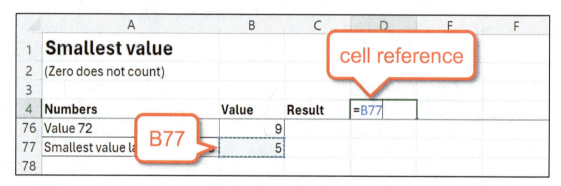

Or: You can also type in the cell reference by hand.
4. Confirm the entry with the ***enter key*** ⏎ and look at the result.

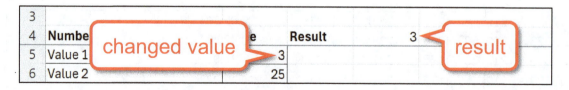

Result: The result is also displayed in cell D4.
5. Enter the value *3* in B5 and look at the result.

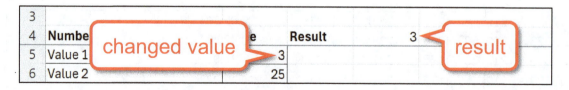

Result: After the input, 3 is the smallest value in the list. Zero is not considered.
Advice: The following rule applies when linking cells: First enter an equal sign in the cell that is to display the value. Then click on the cell that already contains the desired text or value. Then confirm with the ***enter key*** ⏎.
6. Save the file and close Excel.

91 Linking cells 2

These instructions describe how you can link the content of a cell to a cell in another table sheet.

Instruction

1. Open the sample file: ***Chapter 91 - Shoes - Start - B3***
2. Enter and equal sign (=) in cell ***B4*** in the ***Total*** sheet tab.

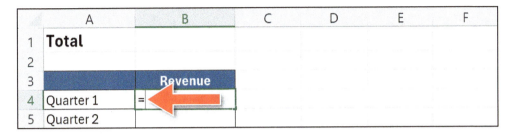

3. Click on the ***Quarter1*** sheet tab to activate this sheet.

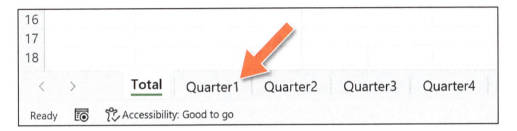

4. Click on cell E11 to create a link to this cell content. Then look at the formula bar.

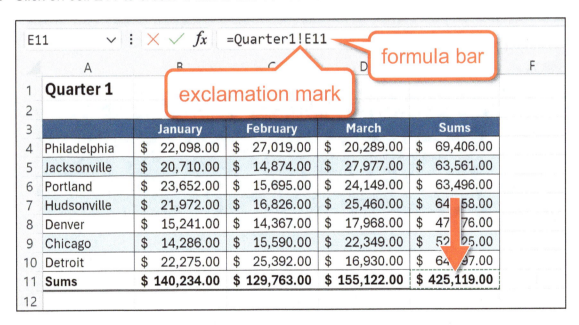

Result: The formula bar shows the formula ***=Quarter1!E11***. This formula is in cell B4 in the ***Total*** sheet tab.

Advice: The exclamation mark separates the name of the sheet from the name of the cell.

Attention: If there is a space in the name of the sheet, the name of the sheet would be placed in quotation marks ('). The formula would be as follows: ***='Quarter 1'!E11***

5. Press the **enter key** ⏎ to confirm the entry. Do <u>not</u> click on the **Total** sheet. Look at the result.

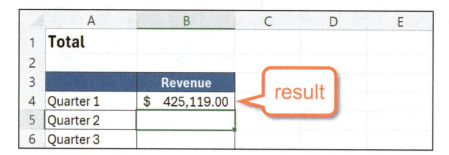

Attention: If you click on the **Total** tab in this situation, the formula will be changed again. It would read: **=Total!E11**. This is a very common error in this step. Press the enter key immediately after clicking on E11.

Result: Excel switches back to the **Total** sheet and displays the result of cell E11. Edit mode is ended.

Advice: The cell with which you create a link in this example is in a different sheet tab. However, the rule for linking cells remains the same (see previous chapter). It is as follows: First enter an equal sign in the cell that is to display the value. Then click on the cell that already contains the desired text or value. Confirm the selection immediately with the **enter key** ⏎. The only difference in this situation is that you must click on the sheet tab containing the value after the equal sign.

6. Change a value in the **Quarter1** sheet and check the change in the **Total** sheet tab.

   Result: Cell B4 in the **Total** sheet tab shows the current result.

7. Also create linking cells for the 3 other quarters in the **Total** sheet tab.

8. Save the file and close Excel.

Dear reader,

ityco is a small company. Please consider supporting us by reviewing this book on Amazon.

With kind regards, Peter Kynast ♥

You can submit your review in your Amazon orders with a single click. Even if you did not buy the book yourself, you can still leave a review. Search "Peter Kynast" on Amazon and click on "Write a costumer review" on the product page. You can also scan this QR-Code, it will take you to the review page.

92   Changing the reference type with F4

In Excel, there are relative, mixed and absolute references. You can recognize mixed and absolute references by the dollar sign ($). The dollar sign is used to specify the numbers or letters of the references. These instructions describe how you can change the reference type.

Instruction

1. Open the sample file: ***Chapter 92 - Markup - Start - B3***
2. Enter the formula ***=B6*B3*** in cell C6. However, do not complete the entry yet.

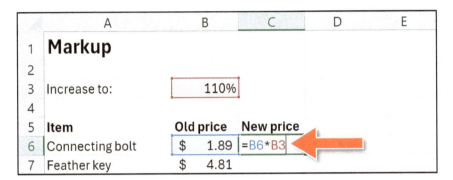

Advice: The formula should then be copied downwards. The reference to cell B3 must therefore not change.

3. Press the ***function key*** F4 to change the reference type.

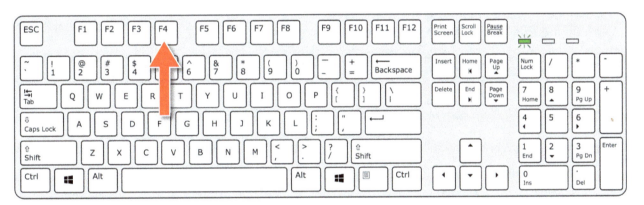

4. Look at the result.

Result: An absolute reference is inserted. A dollar sign is inserted before the letter and the number.
Advice: As this formula is then copied downwards, a dollar sign in front of the number is sufficient. The dollar before the letter has no effect when copied the formula downwards.

5. Press the ***function key*** F4 again to change the reference type.
   Result: The reference is changed to ***=B6*B$3***.
6. Confirm the entry and copy the formula to the cells below.
7. Save the file and close Excel.

---

93   Converting old Excel files

With Excel 2007, Microsoft has changed the Excel file format. The file format determines which techniques, formats and functions can be saved in an Excel file. In older Excel files, you have significantly fewer options than in the new file format. For example, you cannot save smart tables or conditional formatting in them. You should therefore convert old files to the new file format. If you want to keep the old file, make a copy beforehand.

Instruction

1. Open the sample file: ***Chapter 93 - Garden supplies - Start - B3***
2. Look at the title bar.

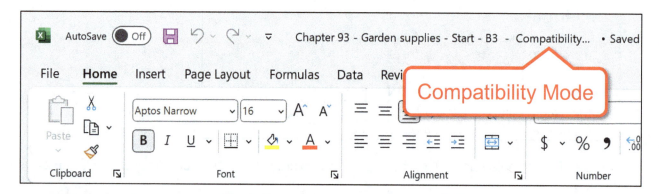

Result: The addition ***Compatibility Mode*** is displayed after the file name. This tells you that this is a file in the old file format.

3. Click on the ***File*** tab → ***Info*** → ***Convert***.

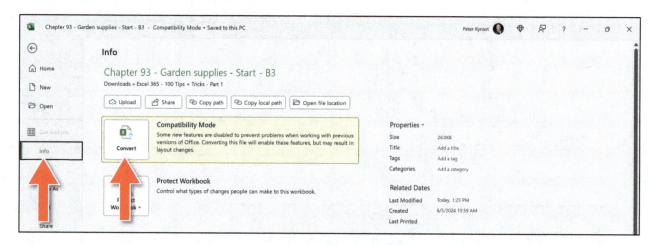

Result: A message is displayed. You will be informed that the file will be saved in the new file format and the old file will be deleted.

4. Confirm the message with the ***OK*** button to carry out the process.
    Result: Another message informs you that the conversion has been completed. You will be asked whether Excel should close and reopen the file now. Only then can you edit the new file.
5. Confirm this message with the ***Yes*** button to close and reopen the workbook.
    Result: The file is closed and opened. The addition ***Compatibility Mode*** is no longer displayed. You can now use and save all techniques in the file.
6. Close Excel without saving.
    Advice: The file has already been saved during the conversion to the new file format.

94   Quickly copying a spreadsheet

To copy a spreadsheet, you can use the right mouse button. However, this process takes a long time as involves several clicks. These instructions describe how you can copy a spreadsheet much faster.

Instruction

1. Open the sample file: ***Chapter 94 - Camping items - Start - B3***
2. Press and hold the ***control key*** Ctrl .
3. Click on the ***Quarter 1*** sheet tab and drag the mouse a little to the right.

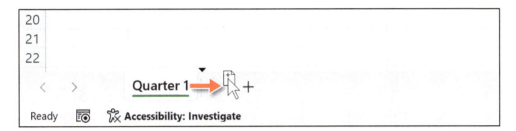

4. Release the mouse button first and then the ***control key*** Ctrl to copy the spreadsheet.
5. Look at the result.

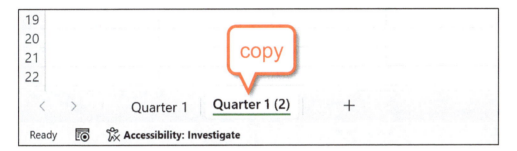

Result: The ***Quarter 1*** spreadsheet has been copied. It is given the name suffix (2), as all sheet tabs must have a unique name.

6. Double-click on the copied sheet tab and change the name to ***Quarter 2***.

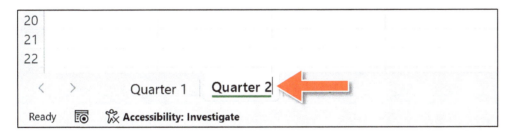

Advice: If you press the ***right arrow key*** → after double-clicking, you undo the selection and do not have to rewrite the whole name.

7. Press the ***enter key*** ↵ to confirm the entry.
    Or: Click on any cell to exit write mode and save the changes to the name.
8. Repeat this process and create 2 more sheet tabs with the names ***Quarter 3*** and ***Quarter 4***.
9. Save the file and close Excel.

95 Comparing spreadsheets

These instructions describe how you can compare 2 spreadsheets.

Instruction

1. Open the sample file: *Chapter 95 - Amusement park - B3*
2. Click on the *New Window* button in the *View* tab to open an additional window for this workbook.

3. Look at the title bar of Excel.

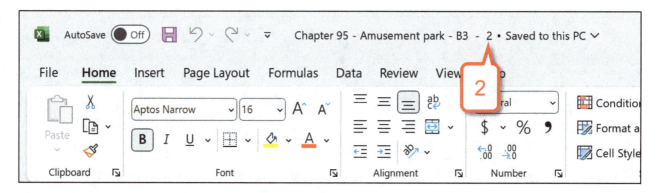

Result: A 2 is displayed after the file name.
Advice: The 2 stands for the second window of this Excel file.
Attention: Depending on the size of your monitor, the title might be cut off and the 2 is not visible. You can also check the full title in the windows taskbar by hovering the mouse over the miniature display of the Excel window to show the full tooltip.

4. Click on the *Arrange All* button in the *View* tab.

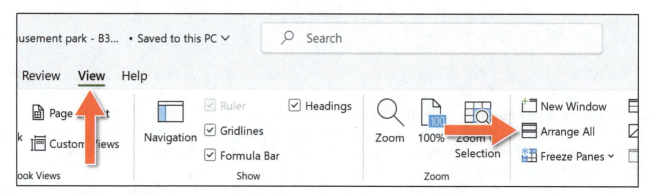

5. Click on the **Vertical** option to display the two windows next to each other.

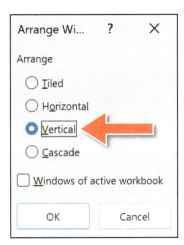

6. Click on the **OK** button and look at the result.

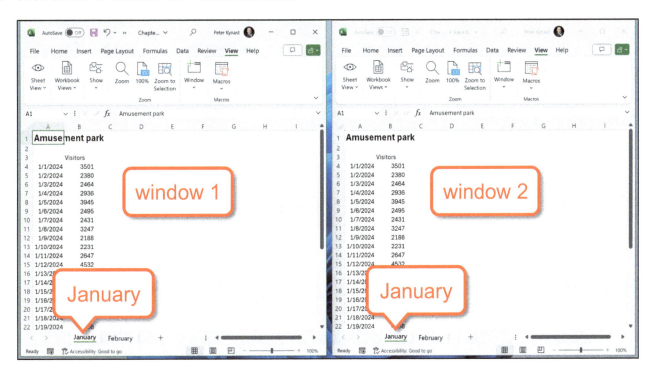

7. Click on the **February** sheet tab in the right-hand window to access this month.

8. Compare the data for the two months and then close both windows.
   Attention: If you change data and close one of the two windows, no saving dialog box will be displayed! The saving dialog boxes only appears when you close the last of the two windows.

96 Using the workbook statistics

These instructions describe how you can access the workbook statistics. They contain helpful information about your current Excel file.

Instruction

1. Open the sample file: **Chapter 96 - Bread sales - B3**
2. Click on the **Workbook Statistics** button in the **Review** tab.

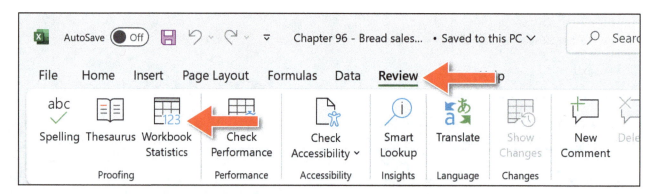

3. Look at the workbook statistics.

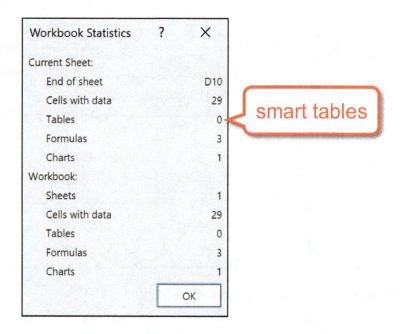

Result: The workbook statistics show you important information about this Excel file. Excel files are also called folders or workbooks.

Advice: The term **sheet** stands for **spreadsheet**. A workbook can contain several sheets. Each sheet has a tab at the bottom of the window. Note the number of tables in this folder. These are the so-called smart tables. This file does not contain any smart tables. This information can be helpful as smart tables are not compatible with all functions. For example, you can no longer use custom views as soon as there is a smart table in the file

4. Close Excel without saving.

97   Sorting columns

These instructions describe how you can sort data that is arranged in columns.

Instruction

1. Open the sample file: **Chapter 97 - Tools - Start - B3**
2. Select the cell range B3 to L30.
3. Click on the **Sort & Filter** button in the **Home** tab.

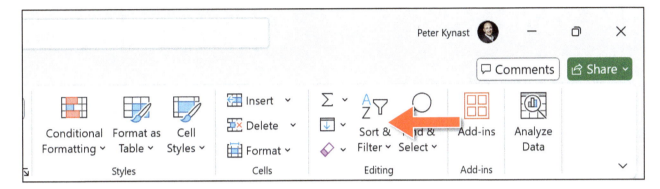

4. Click on the **Custom Sort** list item.

5. Click on the **Options** button in the **Sort** dialog box to access the **Sort Options**.

6. Activate the **Sort left to right** option and click on **OK** to confirm the selection.

7. Select **Row 3** in the **Sort by** list box.

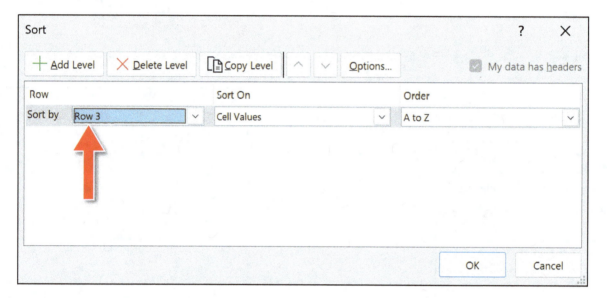

Advice: Row 3 contains the column headings.

8. Confirm the setting by pressing the **OK** button or the **enter key** ⏎ .
9. Undo the selection and look at the result.

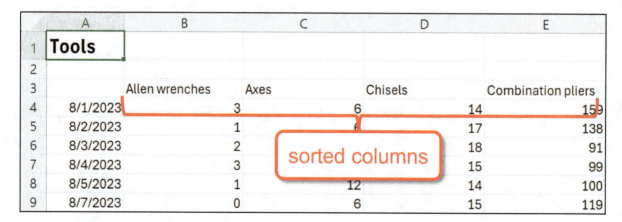

Result: The column headings with the corresponding data were sorted alphabetically.

10. Save the file and close Excel.

© 2024 - www.ityco.com

98 Traces for formulas

Formulas almost always contain cell references and are therefore linked to other cells. These instructions describe how you can make these connections visible using arrows.

Instruction

1. Open the sample file: ***Chapter 98 - Fairgoers - B3***
2. Select cell B4 and click on ***Trace Dependents*** in the ***Formulas*** tab to find cells that calculate with the value in B4.

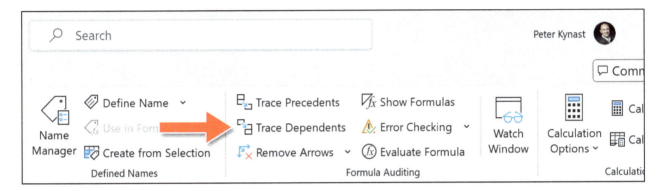

3. Look at the result.

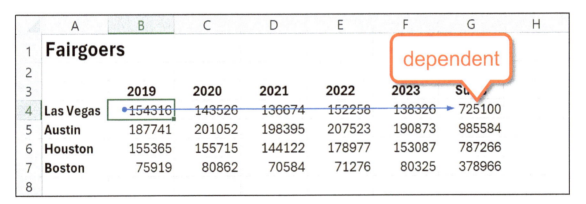

Result: A blue arrow is inserted. It points from B4 to G4.

Advice: In G4 the cells B4 to F4 are added together. G4 is therefore dependent on B4.

4. Click on the ***Remove Arrows*** button in the ***Formulas*** tab to remove the arrow again.

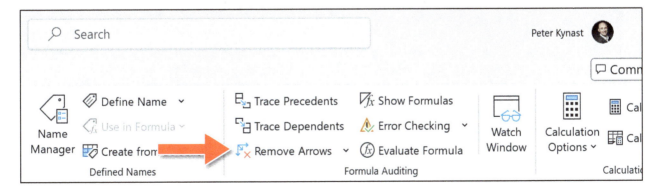

5. Select cell B10 and click on the **Trace Precedents** button.

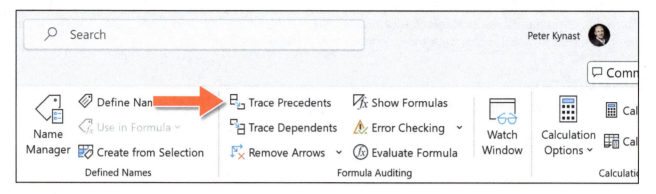

6. Look at the result.

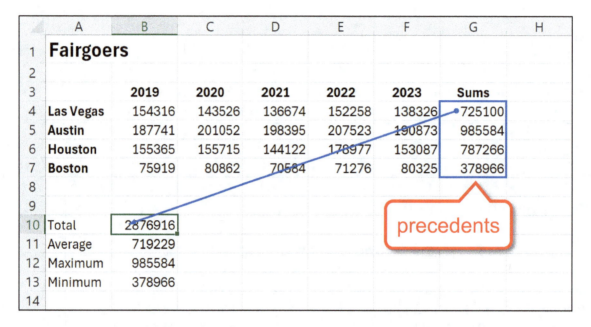

Result: A blue arrow points from G4 to B10. The cells G4 to G7 are displayed with a blue border.
Advice: The sum of G4 to G7 is calculated in B10. G4 to G10 are predecessors of B10 and receive a blue border.

7. Click on the **Remove arrows** button to remove the arrows again.

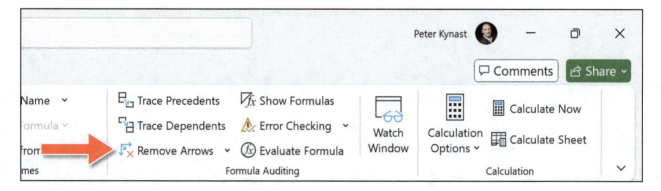

8. Close Excel without saving.

© 2024 - www.ityco.com

99   Header / Footer with file path

These instructions describe how you can display the path to the file in the header or footer of a table. This information makes it easier for colleagues to find original documents that are only available to them as PDF files or printouts.

Instruction

1. Open the sample file: ***Chapter 99 - Vacation request form - Start - B3***
2. Click on the ***Page Layout*** button in the ***View*** tab.

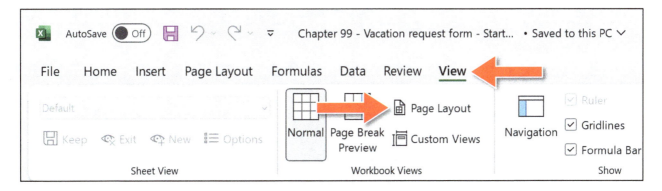

3. Click in the left-hand area of the header to place the cursor there.

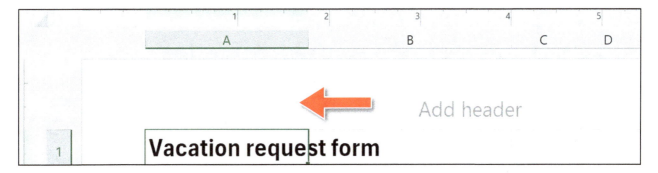

Advice: The header is divided into 3 areas (left, center, right).

4. Look at the result.

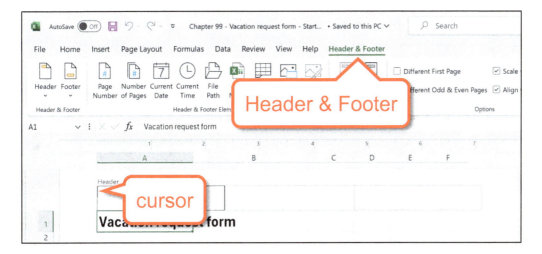

Result: The cursor is placed in the header. At the same time, the ***Header & Footer*** tab is activated.

5. Click on the **File path** button.

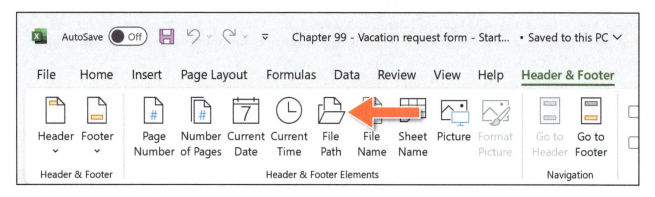

6. Look at the result.

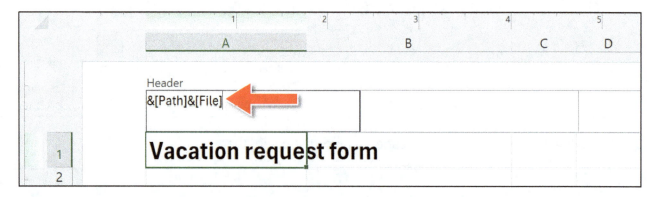

Result: The file path is displayed as the code **&[Path]&[File]** in the left area of the header.

7. Click on the **View** tab and look at the ribbon.

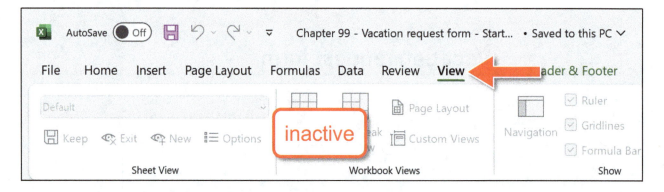

Result: Most of the buttons are inactive. They are therefore displayed in grey.
Advice: In this situation, the behavior of Excel might be irritating. <u>If the cursor is in the header or footer, the buttons in the **View** tab are inactive!</u>

8. Click on any cell in the worksheet.

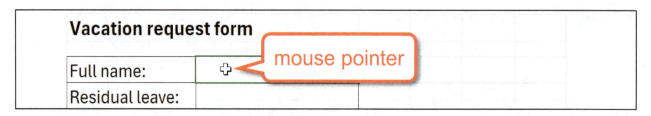

9. Look at the result and then click on the *Normal* view to return to the normal view.

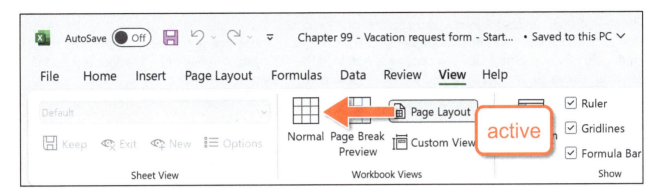

Attention: The buttons are only active again once a cell in the table has been selected.

10. Click on the *File* tab → *Print* to access the print dialog.
11. Look at the result.

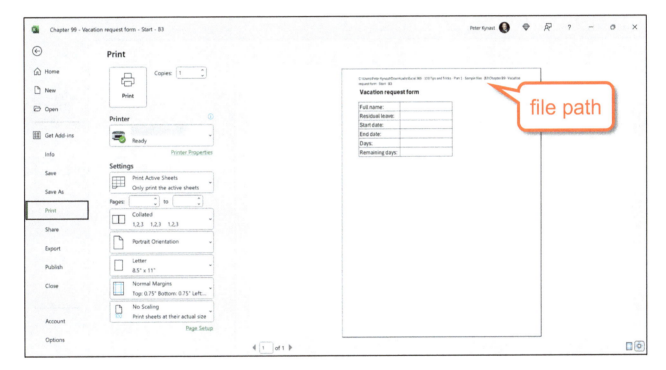

Result: The file path is displayed in the header.

12. Save the file and close Excel.

Compare!

Would you like to compare your exercises? You can find the results in your sample file folder.

100   Displaying the file location

These instructions describe how you can find out the actual file location of an opened excel worksheet. This is helpful if you have opened a file via a shortcut, as in these cases the storage location is not immediately obvious. Shortcuts can occur anywhere in the file system. They are often located on the desktop. However, the list of recently used files also consists of shortcuts.

Instruction

1. Open any Excel file.
2. Click on the *File* tab to open the so-called *Backstage view*.

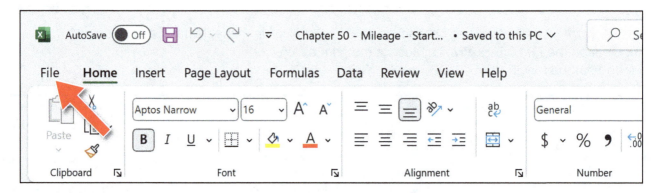

3. Click on the *Info* category and read the file location below the file name.

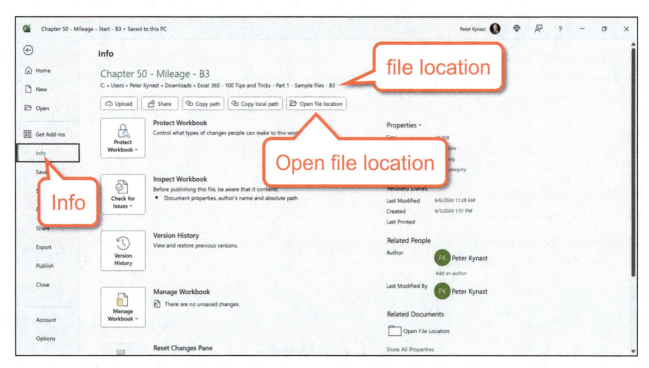

Advice: If you want to open the file location, e.g. to copy the file, click on the ***Open file location*** button. Please note that the file must be closed before copying.

4. Close Excel without saving.

www.ingramcontent.com/pod-product-compliance
Lightning Source LLC
LaVergne TN
LVHW081757050326
832903LV00027B/1984